*The publisher and the University of California Press Foundation
gratefully acknowledge the generous support
of the George Gund Foundation Imprint
in African American Studies.*

Making All Black Lives Matter

AMERICAN STUDIES NOW:
CRITICAL HISTORIES OF THE PRESENT

Edited by Lisa Duggan and Curtis Marez

Much of the most exciting contemporary work in American Studies refuses the distinction between politics and culture, focusing on historical cultures of power and protest on the one hand, or the political meanings and consequences of cultural practices, on the other. *American Studies Now* offers concise, accessible, authoritative, e-first books on significant political debates, personalities, and popular cultural phenomena quickly, while such teachable moments are at the forefront of public consciousness.

Making All Black Lives Matter

Reimagining Freedom in the Twenty-First Century

Barbara Ransby

UNIVERSITY OF CALIFORNIA PRESS

University of California Press, one of the most distin-
guished university presses in the United States, enriches
lives around the world by advancing scholarship in the
humanities, social sciences, and natural sciences. Its
activities are supported by the UC Press Foundation and
by philanthropic contributions from individuals and
institutions. For more information, visit www.ucpress.edu.

University of California Press
Oakland, California

Library of Congress Cataloging-in-Publication Data

Names: Ransby, Barbara, author.
Title: Making all Black lives matter : reimagining
    freedom in the twenty-first century / Barbara Ransby.
Description: Oakland, California : University of
    California Press, [2018] | Includes bibliographical
    references.
Identifiers: LCCN 2018008706 (print) | LCCN 2018012421
    (ebook) | ISBN 9780520966116 (epub and ePDF) |
    ISBN 9780520292703 (cloth : alk. paper) |
    ISBN 9780520292710 (pbk. : alk. paper)
Subjects: LCSH: Black lives matter movement. |
    Black power—United States—History—21st century.
Classification: LCC E185.615 (ebook) | LCC E185.615 .R26 2018
    (print) | DDC 323.1196/073—dc23
LC record available at https://lccn.loc.gov/2018008706

Manufactured in the United States of America

26 25 24 23 22 21 20 19 18
10 9 8 7 6 5 4 3 2 1

When our political activism isn't rooted in a theory about transforming the world, it becomes narrow; when it is focused only on individual actors instead of larger systemic problems, it becomes short-sighted. We do have to deal with the current crisis in the short term. That's important. We have to have solutions for people's real-life problems, and we have to allow people to decide what those solutions are. We also have to create a vision that's much bigger than the one we have right now.

Patrisse Khan-Cullors, cofounder
#BlackLivesMatter

CONTENTS

OVERVIEW

INTRODUCTION

The introduction provides a general survey of the Movement for Black Lives (commonly known as the Black Lives Matter Movement), which will be abbreviated throughout the text as BLMM/M4BL. BLMM/M4BL is a far-reaching movement for racial justice and social transformation (2012–17) that was triggered by vigilante and police violence against Black people in the United States. This chapter also introduces the thesis of the book, which argues that the movement is politically and ideologically grounded in the US-based Black feminist tradition, a tradition that embraces an intersectional analysis while insisting on the interlocking and interconnected nature of different systems of oppression; advocates the importance of women's group–centered leadership; supports LGBTQIA issues; and seeks to center the most marginalized and vulnerable members of the Black community in terms of the language and priorities of the movement.

#BlackLivesMatter · State and Vigilante Violence ·
Black Feminist Intersectional Praxis · Anti-Black Racism

CHAPTER 1. ROOTS AND RECALIBRATED EXPECTATIONS

This chapter offers short biographical profiles of a handful of BLMM/M4BL leaders and founders and traces the antecedents of the Movement for Black Lives in other feminist-centered and Black radical organizations that have focused on state violence. Key groups and campaigns surveyed include Black HIV/AIDS mobilization of the 1990s; the Black Radical Congress; INCITE! Women of Color against Violence; and the prison abolitionist group Critical Resistance. The election of Barack Obama, the nation's first African American president, another precursor to the emergence of BLMM/M4BL, is also explored in this chapter, which argues that BLMM/M4BL represents a rejection of "postracialism" and the middle-class "politics of respectability" that surrounded the Obama presidency. Rather, racism for the majority of poor and working-class Black people, despite the election of a Black president, is far from over.

Black Radical Congress · *Critical Resistance* · *INCITE! Women of Color against Violence* · *Prison-Industrial Complex* · *Barack Obama*

CHAPTER 2. JUSTICE FOR TRAYVON

The 2012 killing of unarmed Florida teenager Trayvon Martin triggered a series of protests and inspired the formation of a number of groups—namely, Black Youth Project 100 (BYP100), Million Hoodies, Dream Defenders, and the Black Lives Matter Global Network—that played prominent roles in BLMM/M4BL as it evolved. This chapter outlines the origins of those groups, as well as the birth of the Free Marissa Now campaign, which demanded the fair treatment of a woman who was jailed despite her claim of self-defense. Her case demonstrated the important feminist principle that women victims of state injustice should be supported and mourned alongside men.

Trayvon Martin · *Black Lives Matter Global Network* · *BYP100 (Black Youth Project 100)* · *Million Hoodies Movement for Justice* · *Dream Defenders* · *Marissa Alexander*

CHAPTER 3. THE FERGUSON UPRISING
AND ITS REVERBERATIONS

The August 2014 uprising in Ferguson, Missouri, that followed the police murder of eighteen-year-old Michael Brown is often cited as the catalyst for the emergence of a full-blown, Black-led resistance movement. It reverberated around the world and garnered intensive news and social media coverage. This chapter chronicles the Ferguson protests, the conditions that spawned them, and the organizers and activists who led and sustained them, notably young Black women, some of them queer and many of whom found their feminist sensibilities and politics crystallized by the uprising.

Ferguson Uprising · Michael Brown · Organization for Black Struggle · MAU (Millennial Activists United) · Movement for Black Lives · Lost Voices

CHAPTER 4. BLACK RAGE AND BLACKS IN POWER

The death of Freddie Gray, a twenty-five-year-old Black man in police custody, triggered the second major uprising in less than a year's time. This chapter covers the Baltimore protests, key activist organizations, and the significant fact that half of the police officers and many of the local authorities involved were Black. BLMM/M4BL organizers indicted the system in Baltimore as racist, emphasizing the structural nature of the problems that persisted, irrespective of which individuals were carrying out policy. The chapter concludes with a lesser-known Baltimore story, that of Korryn Gaines. Gaines was a young mother killed by police in her own home, whose death also sparked protests and debates about gender and self-defense. Baltimore protesters and Gaines's defenders were angry, not only about what occurred in Baltimore but about the cumulative impact of the multiple high-profile police killings of unarmed Black people that had taken place since Michael Brown's death in Ferguson. The chapter also explores how writers and activists have talked about the politics of rage and outrage.

Freddie Gray · Korryn Gaines · Leaders of a Beautiful Struggle · Baltimore United for Change

CHAPTER 5. THEMES, DILEMMAS, AND CHALLENGES

Chapter 5 warns against seeing the movement as monolithic by teasing out and briefly highlighting five distinct but interrelated themes that have arisen as BLMM/M4BL has evolved: the emphasis on "blackness" and Black oppression, as reflected in the slogan "Unapologetically Black"; the role of social media and social media personalities; the youth-centered nature of the movement and the intergenerational politics that have surrounded it; sexism within the movement and new Black feminist and abolitionist-informed practices that seek to hold activists accountable for sexist behavior; and finally the class politics of the movement and leaders' critique of racial capitalism.

Unapologetically Black · Postracialism · Black Twitter · Black Feminism · #SAYHERNAME · #cutthecheck

CHAPTER 6. BACKLASH AND A PRICE

This chapter touches upon the ways in which BLMM/M4BL has been a target of threats, excessive punishment by the state, and disparaging and defamatory statements from conservative politicians and pundits, as well as how its own internal stresses and losses have jeopardized the movement. The shootings of BLMM/M4BL protestors in Minnesota, the arrest of Jasmine Abdullah Richards, the long jail term for Josh Williams in St. Louis, and the suicide of one of the movement's young leaders in Ohio are all part of the price that organizers have paid over the course of the past few years as this movement has unfolded.

Black Friday 14 · Mall of America Protests · Jasmine Abdullah Richards · Josh Williams · MarShawn McCarrel

CHAPTER 7. A VIEW FROM THE LOCAL

This chapter focuses on one local political ecosystem, the City of Chicago, where BLMM/M4BL organizations have been very active and, to a certain extent, successful in campaigning against police and state violence targeting Black communities. The Chicago case study outlines several key campaigns and offers short biographical sketches of individuals and organizations that have been catalysts for change in the city. In addition to the national organizations already mentioned, local groups like the short-lived We Charge Genocide collective, the Let Us Breathe Collective, and Assata's Daughters have helped to anchor the activist work in Chicago, building upon long-standing traditions of organizing and activism in the Black community. Three of the movement's important achievements have been the firing of the police chief, the electoral defeat of an unsympathetic state's attorney, and the victory of a reparations ordinance for survivors of police torture.

Jon Burge Torture Scandal · Justice for Rekia ·
Laquan McDonald · #ByeAnita · We Charge Genocide ·
Let Us Breathe Collective · Assata's Daughters

CHAPTER 8. POLITICAL QUILTERS AND MAROON SPACES

Building organizations is different from building a broad-based social movement that includes multiple organizations. Chapter 8 focuses on Blackbird, a strategic and communications team dedicated to movement-building that was formed in the wake of Ferguson; BOLD (Black Organizing for Leadership and Dignity), a small nonprofit leadership-development and network-building group; and the BlackOUT Collective, a group of tactical and direct action trainers. These three groups (or political quilters) have been instrumental in "stitching together" different patches of BLMM/M4BL work through workshops, leadership training, political education, strategic convenings, and tactical training and support. They have also provided the scaffolding that structures a movement made up of dozens of local and national formations. Each of the three groups has played a different role, but their net effect has been to supply the connective tissue that has turned an assemblage of organizations into a movement. I use the metaphor of maroonage to highlight the ways in which "political quilters" have allowed activists to retreat from intensive periods and spaces of organizing to reflect, connect with one another, and refuel.

Blackbird · BOLD (Black Organizing for Leadership and
Dignity) · BlackOUT Collective · Political Quilting

CONCLUSION

The conclusion briefly situates BLMM/M4BL in the context of a shifting political landscape and of a large and long Black radical history. From a discussion of the prison abolitionist politics of Ruth Gilmore, to the legacy of the 1970s Black feminist group the Combahee River Collective, to the hostile political climate that arose in the wake of the election of Donald Trump as president, this chapter explores BLMM/ M4BL's current challenges and possible trajectory.

Racial Capitalism · Abolition · Nonreformist Reforms · Intersectionality

EPILOGUE

These final pages offer my very personal reflections as a participant-observer in BLMM/M4BL for over two years. As a historian, I had never written about a movement in the making, and I found it a uniquely powerful, moving, and challenging experience. In the epilogue, I take off my researcher's hat and share deeply personal observations and sentiments about BLMM/M4BL and what I observed in the process of writing its story.

Protofascism · Aislinn Pulley · Bree Newsome · Mary Hooks

Introduction

Black Lives Matter began as a social media hashtag in 2013 in response to state and vigilante violence against Black people, sparked by the vigilante murder of Trayvon Martin in Sanford, Florida, 2012, and the police murder of Michael Brown in Ferguson, Missouri, 2014. The slogan has evolved into the battle cry of this generation of Black youth activists. Tens of thousands of people participated in Black Lives Matter protests in some form between 2013 and 2017. At the height of the protests a Pew poll indicated that over 40 percent of Americans were sympathetic to the Black Lives Matter movement, as they understood it.[1] In the same period, the term *Black Lives Matter* was tweeted over a hundred thousand times per day.[2] There is hardly a person in the United States who has not heard the now ubiquitous phrase.

The breadth and impact of *Black Lives Matter* the term has been extraordinary. It has penetrated our consciousness and our lexicon, from professional sports to prime time television, to corporate boardrooms, and to all sectors of the art world. The powerful phrase has resonated as a moral challenge, and as a slap in the face, to the distorting and deceptive language of colorblindness and postracialism that gained traction in the United States after voters elected the country's first African American president in November 2008. While the symbolism was powerful, having a Black man in the White House as president did not change the material reality for some thirteen million Black people living in the United States—a reality that included economic inequality, the epidemic of mass incarceration, and various forms of unchecked state violence. The protest and transformative justice movement that emerged under the banner of the Black Lives Matter Movement (BLMM), and later the Movement for Black Lives (M4BL), rejected representative politics as a stand-in for substantive change in the condition of Black people's lives. The 2014 uprising in Ferguson, Missouri, was not the beginning of that fight, but it was a pivot.

What are the forces, who are the individuals, and what are the underlying ideas that have animated, nurtured, and sustained this movement? The answer is complicated, but one important fact stands out. Black feminist politics have been the ideological bedrock of Black Lives Matter and the Movement for Black Lives. Black women have been prominent in leadership and as spokespersons, and have insisted on being recognized as such. The movement has also addressed the racism and violence experienced by the LGBTQIA communities. Organizers have enacted a Black feminist intersectional praxis in the campaigns, documents, and vision of the major BLMM/M4BL organizations.[3] And it is important to note that while Black feminist ideas had influenced many veteran BLMM/M4BL organizers before they entered this phase of the movement, these ideas have also circulated widely among new activists and protesters, giving women (and men) who had not previously been introduced to

Black feminism an entry point and a larger vision for change and transformation. The new activists have encountered Black feminist terms and concepts like *intersectionality* in the context of struggle, rather than simply through textbooks or in college classrooms. Finally, BLMM/M4BL organizations have championed a grassroots, group-centered approach to leadership very much akin to the teachings of Black Freedom Movement icon Ella Baker (1903–86).

This movement has also patently rejected the hierarchical hetero-patriarchal politics of respectability. Organizers have eschewed values that privilege the so-called best and brightest, emphasizing the needs of the most marginal and often-maligned sectors of the Black community: those who bear the brunt of state violence, from police bullets and batons to neoliberal policies of abandonment and incarceration. Black feminist politics and sensibilities have been the intellectual lifeblood of this movement and its practices. This is the first time in the history of US social movements that Black feminist politics have defined the frame for a multi-issue, Black-led mass struggle that did not primarily or exclusively focus on women. I use the term *Black-led mass struggle* because it is decidedly not a Black-only struggle, and it is not only for Black liberation but rather contextualizes the oppression, exploitation, and liberation of Black poor and working-class people within the simple understanding, at least in the US context, that "once all Black people are free, all people will be free." In other words, poor Black people are represented in all categories of the oppressed in the United States. They are immigrants. They are poor and working class. They are disabled. They are indigenous. They are LGBTQIA. They are Latinx and Afro-Asians. They are also Muslim and other religious minorities, and the list goes on. So to realize the liberation of "all" Black people means undoing systems of injustice that impact all other oppressed groups as well.

In addition to being distinct in its inclusivity, this new movement is defined by action—street protests, uprisings, and various forms of direct action—and it is at its heart a visionary movement, calling not only for reforms but for systemic and fundamental change. Many of its participants identify as abolitionists, imagining a world without prisons or police. Others envision lives without the sanctions and violence that attempt to regulate their bodies, their gender expressions, and their sexuality. And others still dare to imagine a postcapitalist society in which competition, greed, gross wealth disparity, and various forms of waste and excess do not rule the day and the billionaire class do not rule over all of us. In the spirit of Black literary genius James Baldwin, they are "demanding the impossible," or the seemingly impossible.

Even though "Black Lives Matter" is how the movement has been most commonly referenced, the Black Lives Matter Global Network (BLMGN) is only one organization within a larger constellation of groups that fall under the Movement for Black Lives (M4BL), which is both an umbrella term and a coalition that includes dozens of local and national organizations. For purposes of inclusivity I will use the combined term—Black Lives Matter Movement and the Movement for Black Lives (BLMM/M4BL)—to refer to the movement as a whole encompassing both affiliated and unaffiliated forces that have emerged or gained traction post-2012, through their protests and organizing efforts against anti-Black racism, especially as it manifests in various forms of police, state, and vigilante violence. When referring to specific organizations only, I will use those specific organizational names.[4]

BLMM/M4BL includes an assemblage of dozens of organizations and individuals that are actively in one another's orbit, having collaborated, debated, and collectively employed an array of tactics together: from bold direct actions to lobbying politicians and creating detailed policy documents—most notably, the "Vision for Black Lives" platform, released in August 2016. It also includes a mass base of followers and supporters, who may not be formally affiliated with any of the lead organizations but are supportive of and sympathetic toward the spirit of the movement and are angered by the practices, policies, and events that sparked it. The different sectors don't always agree, and there have been some partings of the ways, but for the most part there is a sense of camaraderie—that they are a political family with a critical core holding them together. Most of the organizations are now part of the M4BL coalition founded in December 2014.

The origin story of the Twitter hashtag #BlackLivesMatter has been well documented. In the wake of George Zimmerman's acquittal for the killing of unarmed Black teenager Trayvon Martin in Florida in 2012, Oakland-based activist Alicia Garza, like millions of others, was heartbroken, frustrated, and angry when she wrote what she termed a love letter to Black people, ending it with a version of the phrase "Black Lives Matter (BLM)." She then joined forces with two sister-activists, Opal Tometi and Patrisse Cullors (now Patrisse Khan-Cullors), to create a hashtag and social media platform under that same banner. The term took off on Twitter and Facebook in August 2014 with the rise of collective action in Ferguson, Missouri.[5]

Trayvon Martin's murder in 2012 and Zimmerman's acquittal in 2013 sparked nationwide protests; however, it was in the context of the police killing of unarmed teenager Michael Brown in Ferguson, Missouri, in August 2014, and the widely televised and tweeted mass protests that followed, that the slogan Black Lives Matter migrated from the virtual world of social media to the real politics of the street. Millions around the world watched searing images on television and social media as a small midwestern Black community stood up to state violence, and the devaluation of Black life, in a way the world had not seen in decades.[6]

The Ferguson uprising, an organic mass rebellion sparked by Brown's death at the hands of a member of a notoriously racist local police force, was a defining moment for the early twenty-first-century Black Freedom struggle. Hundreds of people took to the streets and made them their own. They defied state power and exposed what many outside the Black community would rather ignore—the violent underbelly of racial capitalism and systemic racism. And the police did indeed show their true colors by firing teargas and rubber bullets and rough-handling peaceful demonstrators. In the summer and fall of 2014, Ferguson became the epicenter of not only Black resistance but resistance to the neoliberal state and its violent tactics of suppression and control.[7] It was evident that, while Brown's killing was the catalyst, the Black working class of Ferguson was angry about much more, and their anger resonated and reverberated around the country and beyond.

Three weeks after the Ferguson uprising began, Patrisse Khan-Cullors teamed up with activist Darnell Moore to organize #BLM's online followers to conduct solidarity freedom rides that would lend support to the protesters in Ferguson. Over five hundred heeded the call. The Black Lives Matter Network, later the BLMGN, grew out of that action. As of spring 2017, it had forty-three chapters in three countries (the United States, the United Kingdom, and Canada), a small paid staff, and a global profile.[8] But the Black Lives Matter Network and its outgrowth, the BLMGN, are only part of the story.

In parallel, and in some cases even before the formation of the BLMGN, other national and regional organizations were formed that were absolutely central to the movement organizing that has unfolded. They include the Chicago-based national Black Youth Project 100 (BYP100), with an engaged membership of young adults between eighteen and thirty-five years old, in chapters around the country; the Dream Defenders, a people of color–led multiracial group in Florida; the St. Louis–based Organization for Black Struggle; and Million Hoodies Movement for Justice, a people of color–led multiracial national group based in New York City.[9]

In addition, there is a whole ecosystem of local organizations that either emerged or grew larger in size and influence in response to killing after killing after killing: Leaders of a Beautiful Struggle in Baltimore, the Justice League in New York (founded before 2014), and the Let Us Breathe Collective in Chicago. Ferguson itself gave rise to Millennial Activists United, Tribe X, Hands Up United (led by charismatic young poet-activist Tef Poe), and Lost Voices (a group formed literally through protest encampments on the streets of Ferguson in the thick of the uprising.) The list goes on.

There is also a third tier of relatively new movement organizations that are serving a very special function. They nurture, sustain, and support base-building organizations while at the same time connecting them to one another through new movement infrastructures, a network of relationships, and a growing movement culture. These groups, which are less visible, often operating under the radar of the public, are doing a kind of "political quilting" that seeks to bolster awareness across movement work. They function in the interstitial spaces between organizations, providing political education and skills and tactical training while navigating the temporal spaces between high and low periods of movement activity.[10]

In the twenty-first-century BLMM/M4BL moment, there are three very different groups that play the role of political quilters. They are the Blackbird team; the leadership-training organization BOLD (Black Organizing for Leadership and Dignity), based largely in Miami; and the Oakland-centered BlackOUT Collective. Each group has a distinctive history and its own unique role in movement-support work. All three embrace, in one way or another, a Black feminist ethos and politics, and Black feminist women and LGBTQIA folk are prominent in their leadership.

Incidents of police violence and other forms of state and vigilante violence were the catalysts for the upsurge in Black resistance between 2014 and 2016, replicating the primary trigger mechanism for Black rebellion throughout the twentieth century. Protests were sparked and accelerated by roughly a dozen high-profile police killings over an extraordinarily intense two-year period, but they are part of a much longer trajectory.[11] Police violence and the lack of accountability were at the center of much of the protesters' anger, but the list of demands, and the overall analysis of most movement organizations, is far more expansive. Movement organizers have pointed out that the lack of affordable housing, low wages, the erosion of public services, the lack of jobs, and spiraling personal debt have all facilitated the slow death of tens of thousands of Black people deemed disposable to this labor-"light" economy of twenty-first-century racial capitalism, to which many are increasingly superfluous.

The election of racist and misogynist demagogue Donald Trump as the forty-fifth president of the United States in November 2016 represented an indirect backlash against the radical antiracism of BLMM/M4BL. This new administration in

Washington, with all of its belligerence and appeals to white nationalists, also challenged and impacted the movement in unexpected ways, catapulting it into a new phase of activity focused on broad-based united front and coalition work. In early 2017, the M4BL coalition was the catalyst for a cross-movement campaign under the rubric "Beyond the Moment," which both marked the fiftieth anniversary of Dr. Martin Luther King Jr.'s historic anti-imperialist "Beyond Vietnam" speech and called for new strategies of resistance. It was launched by M4BL and anchored by the staff of Blackbird. As of December 2017, Beyond the Moment had evolved into a new coalition called "The Majority," which is still in formation as we go to press with this book.

So five years after Trayvon Martin's murder, this book takes stock and takes the pulse of a movement that is still very much alive but is in transition. It does not purport to be comprehensive. Rather it is an analytical overview of the evolving BLMM/M4BL that will hopefully provide the basis for further research, discussion, debate, and organizing. This is not a book about police killings but about the responses to them. It is about the central role of visionary young Black activists who, inspired by Black feminist teachings and practice, are embracing new modes of leadership as they attempt to build a movement that creates transformative possibilities.

In compiling material for this book, I have relied on personal interviews with participants in the movement; traditional and social media archives; government and civil rights reports; and an informal collection of flyers, speeches, descriptions of public programs, and other unprocessed material and ephemera, from individual organizers and activists, in the author's possession. I have also relied on my own experiences as a participant-observer at dozens of meetings, rallies, retreats, and think tanks, as well as on personal conversations. I have taken meticulous care not to violate any confidences or expose any material that would undermine the ongoing work to which I remain committed. I am confident that I have adhered to this principle without compromising the truth-telling mission of the book.

Five recently published books have also been important resources. They are Jamala Rogers's firsthand account of the Black struggle in St. Louis and Ferguson, *Ferguson Is America: Roots of Rebellion;* Keeanga-Yamahtta Taylor's *From #BlackLives-Matter to Black Liberation;* Angela Y. Davis's *Freedom Is a Constant Struggle: Ferguson, Palestine, and the Foundations of a Movement;* Jordan T. Camp and Christina Heatherton's edited collection, *Policing the Planet: Why the Policing Crisis Led to Black Lives Matter;* and Patrisse Khan-Cullors and asha bandele's *When They Call You a Terrorist: A Black Lives Matter Memoir.* Forthcoming books by Charlene Carruthers and Alicia Garza will undoubtedly shed more light on this important social movement. I express my gratitude to all of these authors—people whom I respect as friends and comrades—as well as to scholars and movement intellectuals. Most important, my gratitude goes to the leaders of BLMM/M4BL for their courage, tenacity, creativity, perseverance, and heart.

ONE

Roots and Recalibrated Expectations

Prologue to a Movement

No movement emerges out of thin air. There is always a prologue, and a prologue to the prologue. In other words, there is always a set of conditions and circumstances that set the stage for movements to emerge. Some of that stage-setting is historical, having little to do with the activists and organizers themselves but rather with the political and economic climate and an array of social realities beyond their immediate control. But then there is human agency: what we as human beings, as oppressed people, as conscientious allies of the oppressed, do (or don't do) in response to the conditions and circumstances we encounter. Nothing is predetermined or dictated by history. However, historical conditions both create and limit possibilities for change. And all individual participants in this moment may not even be fully aware of the history on which they stand. Nevertheless, it is there. What is also there is an ever-shifting political reality that, in this case, includes the 2008 election of the nation's first Black president and its implications for Black organizing.

So what is the political genealogy of the Black Lives Matter Movement/Movement for Black Lives (BLMM/M4BL)? In the 1990s, the HIV/AIDS epidemic ravaged vulnerable populations worldwide, including Black gay men and Black intravenous drug users. In the United States, organizations emerged, often led by Black gay men and lesbians, that were intent on challenging the devastation of AIDS in Black communities but also on recognizing Black LGBTQIA folk in our communities. Organizations from Bebashi in Philadelphia to the Minority AIDS Project in Los Angeles, to the National Coalition of Black Lesbians and Gays, to the National Minority AIDS Council all rose up to respond to the suffering of Black people at the center of the epidemic and to insist upon recognizing the voices and leadership of Black gay/queer folk in the fights against HIV/AIDS and for access to treatment. People like Essex Hemphill, Pat Parker, Craig G. Harris, Cheryl Clark, Barbara Smith, Joseph Beam, Gary Paul, and filmmaker Marlon Riggs, to name just a few, through their activism and art manifested the radical Black queer politics that many members of BLMM/M4BL now embrace. Cathy Cohen, herself a leader of the Black AIDS Mobilizations (BAM), points out that the central role Black feminists and Black gay/queer activists play is essential to the Black radical tradition and is too often left out. This erasure, she insists, "must be corrected."[1] This legacy is a part of the political roots of BLMM/M4BL.

In August 2005, Katrina, a devastating category 5 hurricane, hit the southern Gulf coast of the United States, including the historic, predominately Black city of New Orleans. Local officials were ill-prepared, and the federal government under President George W. Bush was callously slow and inept in its response. As a result, thousands were left to suffer and fend for themselves as sewage-contaminated water flooded homes and hospitals and washed away lives and livelihoods. Those suffering and dying in Katrina's wake were disproportionately Black and poor. Americans watched as the US government's blatant disregard for Black pain and death was on full display. As Milwaukee M4BL queer and gender-nonconforming organizer M. Adams put it eloquently, "Katrina and its aftermath felt particularly important to the general conscious-raising of Black folk, and the millennial generation in particular. It in some ways laid the ground to articulate the state's negligence as violent—and it helped folk question what the function of a government/state is. It was an incredible example and symbol of many forms of structural anti-Black racism."[2]

Another critical antecedent to the emergence of BLMM/M4BL goes back to June 1998 and the launch in Chicago of the Black Radical Congress (BRC), a coalition of Black left organizers and intellectuals responding to the devastating impact of neoliberal policies on the Black community, and to the dearth of responsive Black leadership.[3] The BRC revived coalitional Black left organizing, linked disparate radical traditions, made Black feminism central, and confronted white supremacy and racial capitalism head on. Michael Brown was only two years old in 1998. Twitter had not been invented. Facebook was in its infancy. It was another time.

I, along with Manning Marable, Leith Mullings, Bill Fletcher Jr., and Abdul Alkalimat, was one of the founders of the BRC. The concept behind the BRC was to create a Black left pole, as Fletcher described it: to make the Black radical tradition and the Black Left more visible and distinguish it from a mainstream Black political impulse that was invested in representational race politics and the integration of Black elites into existing hierarchies. For Black feminists like myself, the BRC was also a direct response to the 1995 Million Man March, which sought to re-establish the legitimacy of male dominance in Black politics while simultaneously celebrating Black capitalism and patriarchy.[4] We rejected this outright and insisted there was another Black liberation agenda that had to be written and advanced. For many of us that agenda was grounded in Black feminist praxis, one that was multi-issued, anticapitalist, anti-imperialist, and affirming of the full breadth of our humanity and community. The BRC's expansive liberatory agenda was relevant not only to Black women and Black people but to all oppressed people.

In spite of its many mistakes, the BRC was an important landmark in the re-emergence of a new Black Left. One of its most significant achievements is that it managed to bring together the three large, contentious, and sometimes overlapping streams of the Black radical tradition in the US context: Black socialist and communist forces of various stripes, radical Black feminists, and revolutionary nationalists and pan-Africanists. Personalities ranged from a creatively provocative and often irascible poet, Amiri Baraka, to Combahee River Collective cofounder and lesbian feminist leader Barbara Smith. Scholar-activist Cornel West, Communist Party leader Jarvis Tyner, and North Carolina labor activists Rukiya and Ajamu Dillahunt were all active participants. Revolutionary nationalists like Makungu Akinyela, Saladin Muhammad, and Sam Anderson were also in the mix. The unity we achieved in late twentieth-century Black politics by bringing this unlikely cast of characters together was not only unprecedented but, for the time it lasted, principled. That is, it was not simply a coalition of convenience. Under Bill Fletcher Jr.'s able and persistent guidance, the BRC navigated its way through about a half dozen national planning meetings leading up to the congress that was held on the campus of the University of

Illinois at Chicago in June 1998 and that had some two thousand participants. Fletcher's tenacity, vision, and leadership in this effort cannot be overstated. A long-time labor organizer, leftist, and movement strategist, Fletcher saw a political void and was determined to help the BRC fill it. He assuaged egos, crafted potentially divisive unity documents, and chaired a number of unwieldy marathon meetings to hold us together. A significant characteristic of the BRC, as a sixteen-year precursor to BLMM/ M4BL, is its gender politics, which situated a Black feminist intersectional paradigm prominently within the larger frame-work of Black left and radical thought.

The organization's feminist caucus represented a coming together of an amazing intergenerational group of Black feminists, including Cathy Cohen, Lisa Crooms, Sherie Randolph, Lisa Brock, Cheryl I. Harris, Fran Beal, Barbara Smith, Tracye Mat-thews, Leith Mullings, Lynette Jackson, Ashanki Binta, Jamala Rogers, Jennifer Hamer, Helen Neville, and dozens more. Many of the BRC participants became mentors, teachers, allies, advisors, and supporters of the BLMM/M4BL organizers in the 2010s.[5]

Two other organizations are also important parts of the politi-cal tradition from which BLMM/M4BL emerged: Critical Resistance (CR) and INCITE! Women of Color against Vio-lence. The anti–state violence and prison abolition movements of which these groups are a part were largely launched and are led by Black feminists and feminists of color. The role of the two groups in setting the stage for BLMM/M4BL in particular can-not be overstated. These movement organizations, with the visionary demand for prison abolition at their center and their insistence that solutions to violence will not be found in the use of coercive state power, created a language, an analytical frame, a database, and a powerful set of narratives that indict the corrosive and racist nature of the prison-industrial complex (PIC), in which police, sheriff's departments, and other law enforcement entities and carceral projects are embedded. They wrote books, convened conferences, and conducted trainings for a whole generation of activists. Some BLMM/M4BL leaders who are now in their thirties participated in these organizations, and many more read the books and articles written by the radical scholar-activists who led and cofounded INCITE! and CR.

CR was founded in 1997 by Angela Y. Davis, Ruth Wilson Gilmore, and Rose Braz and officially launched in 1998 (the same year as the BRC) in Berkeley, California, at a conference attended by thirty-five hundred people. The group describes its vision this way: "Critical Resistance is building a member-led and member-run grassroots movement to challenge the use of punishment to 'cure' complicated social problems. We know that more policing and imprisonment will not make us safer. Instead, we know that things like food, housing, and freedom are what create healthy, stable neighborhoods and communities. We work to prevent people from being arrested or locked up in prison. In all our work, we organize to build power and to stop the devastation that the reliance on imprisonment and policing has brought to ourselves, our families, and our communities."[6] An understanding of the role of the police, and their often-unchecked power in the larger PIC, is one of the key precepts upon which BLMM/M4BL's anti–police violence political program is built. Prisons, as Davis puts it, facilitate the "disappearing" of people; they are the destination point, the "containers," for the new human chattel. In all of this, the police are the purveyors and enablers of the prison industry, and police violence as a consequence is a critical ingredient in terrorizing communities into submission. The analytical framework of the PIC, a term coined by Mike Davis (no relation to Angela), and popularized and advanced in Angela Davis's 1998 article in the magazine *Colorlines,* helped to set the stage for anti-prison and anti–police violence work in the 2010s.

INCITE!, founded in 2000 and growing out of the anti–domestic violence movement, describes the evolution of its work as follows: "It is impossible to seriously address sexual and intimate partner violence within communities of color without addressing these larger structures of violence (including militarism, attacks on immigrants' rights and Indigenous treaty rights, the proliferation of prisons, economic neo-colonialism, the medical industry, and more). So, our organizing is focused on places where state violence and sexual/intimate partner violence intersect."[7]

A number of books have emerged from INCITE!'s work that have powerfully impacted the current organizing culture and whole generations of feminists of color and others: *Color of Violence: The INCITE! Anthology* (2006) and *The Revolution Will Not Be Funded* (2007), written and edited collectively by INCITE! members; and Beth E. Richie, *Arrested Justice: Black Women, Violence, and America's Prison Nation* (2012). Ruth Wilson Gilmore's landmark book on California's prison system, *Golden Gulag* (2007), and Angela Davis's *Are Prisons Obsolete?* (2003) were also critical foundational texts.[8] These influential publications collectively argue for several things. One is the ways in which overreliance on the state for protection—for example, in cases of domestic violence—has fed the buildup of the carceral state in unexpected ways. Richie cautions against reflexively calling for more arrests and longer prison sentences, even for crimes we deem deplorable, because the way in which police are trained to intervene often makes situations worse and more dangerous when poor Black people are involved. She warns organizers of the trap of foundation funding, which can derail or dilute the intended politics of a given group.[9] And finally, all of these authors stress leadership by those most affected by violence—poor and working-class women of color. The centering of the most marginalized sectors of a community, the critique of prisons and police, and the skepticism about foundation funding have all carried over to the work and values of BLMM/M4BL.

The rise of mass incarceration in the 1990s and early 2000s and of the carceral state, or as Richie terms it, "the prison nation," along with the criminalization of Black bodies, especially those of Black poor, women, and queer folks, laid the political groundwork for the grassroots campaigns and insurgent actions that have characterized the BLMM/M4BL moment. The popular success of Michelle Alexander's 2010 book, *The New Jim Crow: Mass Incarceration in the Age of Colorblindness,* which appeared on the *New York Times* bestseller list for more than a year, though predated by the groundbreaking praxis of INCITE! and CR, nevertheless helped to educate and sensitize a mass audience to the injustices and inhumanity of our current carceral system. Alexander offered her readers the following provocative facts: More Black men were under the control of the criminal justice system in 2010 than had been enslaved in 1850. Even after serving their sentences, mostly for nonviolent drug offenses, former felons are relegated to the status of second-class citizenship in what Alexander calls a "racial caste system," in which they are denied full voting rights, kept under harsh surveillance, excluded from public housing and many student-funding opportunities, and banned from certain jobs.[10] Alexander's widely circulated statistics and compelling language animated the public discourse and furthered public understanding of race, policing, and prisons in the years leading up to 2014.

Angela Davis connected the temporal dots this way in her 2016 book, *Freedom Is a Constant Struggle:* "Over the last two decades I would say, there has actually been sustained organizing against police violence, racism, racist police violence, against prisons, the prison industrial complex, and I think the sustained protests we are seeing now have a great deal to do with that organizing. They reflect the fact that the political consciousness in so many communities is so much higher than people think."[11] Angela Davis herself has done a great deal to advance critical and radical political concerns in specific and deliberate ways. She is a powerful symbol of resistance for this generation of activists, one who has also provided moral and political support to the movement in myriad ways.

It is worthwhile saying a few words about Davis as a legendary figure in Black liberation movement history, and as a Black feminist organizer, because her influence on this generation of activists has been significant. Angela Davis's story and persona in many ways embody the Black radical internationalism of the 1960s and '70s and the radical Black feminism that came a bit later. She first came into public view as a young communist intellectual fired from her teaching job at the University of California by then-governor Ronald Reagan because of her left-wing political views. However, she is best known as a fugitive, and then political prisoner (1970–72), who was wrongly accused of involvement in the failed rescue of another political prisoner—George Jackson, one of the activist Soledad Brothers, who had been her loving friend and comrade. Her iconic Afro and raised fist in the courtroom, in defiance of her captors, became a symbol of Black resistance for an entire generation. "Free Angela" was a movement that circled the globe.

Once an international campaign led to Angela's release in 1972, she dedicated her life's work to prisoner solidarity and prison abolition. She is unapologetic in her feminist, anti-imperialist, and anticapitalist politics. For decades, she has spoken widely and participated in a number of progressive and radical organizations. The announcement that she is going to appear in any given city immediately produces overflow crowds, even at mammoth venues that include many young people. She has a fan club of ardent admirers, to be sure. But the source of her appeal is more than that. More than most other political celebrity figures of the twentieth century, Angela Davis has used her name and her fame in the service of consciousness-raising, mobilizing, and organizing. And she has taken on controversial issues within Black progressive circles: feminist and queer politics, solidarity with Palestine, and prison abolition. She has moved the needle and the consensus on all three. When Angela Davis was a political prisoner in the early 1970s, most BLMM/M4BL organizers had not yet been born. Still, her impact on them is palpable.

Many young activists I have spoken to over the years were introduced to the concepts of the PIC and mass incarceration by listening to, or reading the writings of, Angela Davis. They paid attention *because* she was Angela Davis, but her ideas resonated and were incorporated into their own thinking and organizing. Not surprisingly, Davis was welcomed with open arms when she visited Ferguson two months after the initial uprising. Her collaborative work and her own example have helped to set the stage for the emergence of BLMM/M4BL, with its criticism of state violence, police, hetero-patriarchy, and empire and its open expressions of solidarity with Palestinians, which are reflected in several BLMM/M4BL travel delegations. Davis noted the historical significance of Ferguson when she returned a second time the following year: "Like everyone else who identifies with current struggles against racism and police violence, I have uttered the words 'Ferguson' and 'Michael Brown' innumerable times. Both inside and outside the country—for me as for people throughout the world—the very mention of Ferguson evokes struggle, perseverance, courage, and a collective vision of the future."[12] Davis is on the advisory board of the Dream Defenders.

In terms of mainstream politics, one of the most significant backdrops to the emergence of BLMM/M4BL, and an important factor in understanding its historical significance, was the presidential election of 2008. Many initially considered Barack Obama's election as the nation's first African American president to be a milestone in the long march of racial progress. He won against the odds, with idealistic youth in the forefront, with a progressive populist message, and with legions of young white supporters. However, the dialectic of Obama's victory was a complicated one, as a number of provocative new books on the subject attest.[13] African Americans initially rallied around him, supporting him almost unanimously at the polls and defending him from criticism during his first year or so in office. There was a kind of familial protectiveness of the new commander in chief, as most African Americans struggled in disbelief that he had actually won. Most Black people were simply proud to see a Black man in the White House.

The initial reluctance to criticize Obama by Black communities was also influenced by the nasty racist backlash from the Republicans in Congress and beyond. Obama was immediately the subject of vulgar and unprecedented insults, threats, and attacks on his legitimacy and integrity. Members of the so-called birther movement (led by none other than the now forty-fifth US president, Donald Trump) raised doubts about his citizenship, and many others capitalized on Islamophobia by insinuating that the self-proclaimed Christian was a Muslim (and thus perhaps a terrorist). The list goes on. All of these attacks prompted a defensive reflex in the Black community.

The honeymoon eventually wore off for many, and Black activists confronted the hard reality that simply having a Black family in the White House was not going to save Black families in general. And, moreover, just because Obama was being criticized and attacked from the conservative right did not mean there were no legitimate criticisms to be made by Black people and the Left in general. The ravages of mass incarceration; the erosion of decent-paying union jobs; the evisceration of public services and the overall downsizing of the economy from the 1980s to 2008; and the financial foreclosure crisis hit many Black communities very hard. Added to this were the constant specters of police violence, including harassment, racial profiling, and the killing of Black civilians. Many poor and working-class African Americans were not simply invested in the symbolism of a Black president but had placed hope in his message that resource-draining wars and policies favoring the 1 percent would end and their communities would enjoy tangible benefits. It did not pan out that way. Obama did not deliver. As journalist Jelani Cobb observed, "Until there was a black Presidency it was impossible to conceive of the limitations of one."[14]

Obama's election in 2008 meant many things to many people. Many white liberals hoped the election would represent some form of racial redemption, perhaps secretly hoping that we could be done with race once and for all, or at least that "resolution" of the "race problem" was within our grasp. While no reasonable person could argue that race or racism had been obliterated—that hundreds of years of white supremacy had been swept away in one fell swoop—many wanted to believe that the blatant and unapologetic anti-Black racism of the past had been finally put to rest. To many in the mainstream, the postracial ideal was a seductive one, made all the more visually appealing by the handsome and wholesome, brown-skinned First Family. In addition to white liberals who hoped for a transcendence of race through the Oval Office, Black elites had other hopes and dreams, chief among them that the racial glass ceiling would be cracked, if not broken.

It is important to note that there has indeed been progress for some Black folk. There are more Black millionaires and billionaires, CEOs, and highly paid celebrities than ever before. Still, Black poverty and suffering remain dire. And there is simultaneously greater economic disparity within Black America than ever before. Instead of a trickle down of resources from wealthy Black people to the Black poor, the growth of a more visible, albeit small, Black political and economic elite has obscured the suffering below. If media celebrities like Oprah can earn millions, and politicians like Obama can win the White House, racial barriers to Black progress no longer exist, right? This simplistic and flawed analysis permeated popular discourse in the Obama era.

However, BLMM/M4BL challenged this notion head on. BYP100 director, and a leader in the BLMM/M4BL, Charlene Carruthers described her disillusionment with Obama: "I voted for him when he ran for senate, and I voted for him when he ran for president for the first time. It was with the understanding that there was an optimism and a sentiment of progressivism that his platform at least sought to achieve. And shortly after, there was a wakeup call, again, about the power of politicians in actually transforming society.... And so what I've learned and what I hope many of us learned again are the limitations of any politician to change our lives or to transform our lives."[15] In other words, Carruthers came into BYP100 organizing in 2013 after the murder of Trayvon Martin with diminished expectations about finding solutions through conventional political channels and with diminished confidence in mainstream Black leadership.

Echoing Carruthers's sentiments, St. Louis poet and activist Tef Poe made the following rhetorical appeal in an open letter to the president: "We know you know this is wrong, so the disconnect between your words and your personal convictions has raised many questions in the black community. Now we are organizing against you and members of your party as though we didn't vote for you to begin with. This saddens me, because we rooted for you. We love you and want to sing praises of you to our children, but first we need a statement of solidarity from you to the young black people facing the perils of police brutality. We will not get this statement, and we know it."[16] A coming to terms with the limits of what a Black leader at the helm of this country could, or would, really achieve for the masses of Black people set the stage for the explosion of protests and organizing that began in 2012, reemerged with even greater strength in 2014, and was sustained throughout 2016.

Finally, in addition to the decreased Black confidence in Obama, on the one hand, and the rich political legacy and language of prior Black and people of color–led resistance movements like BRC, CR, and INCITE!, on the other, there was a shift in US politics overall in the years leading up to BLMM/ M4BL that created the possibility for new alliances and a base of progressive white supporters and fellow activists. That shift was represented by the massive Occupy Wall Street (OWS) movement that exposed and challenged wealth disparity, the tyranny of the super-rich 1 percent of the population, and the excesses of capitalism overall. It also revived direct action and civil disobedience tactics as legitimate forms of political expression. Even though there were Black, Latinx, and antiracist white forces within OWS, the movement overall failed to embrace the centrality of race and white supremacy in the matrix of injustice. It remained overwhelmingly white, and whatever antiracist analysis was present was tepid at best.[17] That was a significant weakness.

All of these movements and events nevertheless are important backdrops to BLMM/M4BL. Thousands of white protesters participated in BLMM/M4BL network actions and even initially joined some BLMGN chapters around the country.[18] It is hard to imagine that many of them had not been either part of, or influenced by, OWS in the years prior. As historian and activist Keeanga Yamahtta Taylor points out in her book *From #BlackLivesMatter to Black Liberation,* the 2011 execution in Georgia of Troy Davis, a Black man who many felt was unjustly convicted of murder in 1991, was another watershed moment for this generation of activists. The case inspired a nationwide protest movement and forced many people to take a closer look at the violence inherent in the current criminal justice system.[19]

The individual political histories of key BLMM/M4BL leaders are as important as the earlier campaigns to our understanding of the roots of this movement. The crop of thirty or so BLMM/M4BL lead organizers who have been consistently visible and pivotal to the work at the national level since 2014 have come to the movement with extensive experience in radical grassroots organizing and in the progressive nonprofit worlds. Alicia Garza, for example, worked for P.O.W.E.R. (People Organized to Win Employment Rights), a Bay Area grassroots economic justice group that works to fight gentrification and advocates on behalf of youth. She had participated in a number of progressive and leftist campaigns in the Bay Area before 2014, including the protests after the transit-police shooting of Oscar Grant on New Year's Day 2009. Her job as a director of the National Domestic Workers Alliance continues the long-standing Black feminist charge to fight alongside poor and oppressed women. As a politically engaged queer Black woman married to a transgender man (Malachi Garza, also an activist), she has made LGBTQIA issues central to her larger political worldview and brought those politics with her to BLMGN.[20]

Charlene Carruthers of BYP100 worked for the Women's Media Group and Color of Change before bringing her skills to BYP100. She describes her own political evolution this way: "I grew up on the South Side of Chicago. My family could be best described as working-class. Some of my earliest experiences with power and beginning to understand the kind of world we live in were at the welfare office with my mother, or hearing my father tell stories about people he'd trained receiving promotions over him." And then she visited South Africa on a study abroad program while she was at Illinois Wesleyan University. In her words, that experience in South Africa "expanded my consciousness around what it meant to be Black on a global level."[21]

Born of Nigerian immigrant parents, Opal Tometi learned early on about the combined injustice of colonialism and US-based racism. She emerged as one of the most strident advocates for the rights of Black immigrants within the larger immigrant rights movement years ago, helping to form the Black and Brown Coalition of Arizona in response to the racist, anti-immigrant policies of Maricopa County Sheriff Joe Arpaio. During her time as a college student at the University of Arizona, Opal recalled, "People [undocumented immigrants trying to find safe haven] were dying in the desert just miles from my campus."[22]

She was motivated to get involved, and she did. As of 2017, she continues to serve as executive director of the Black Alliance for Just Immigration, a formidable national organization. It is also significant that before undertaking her work in the immigrant rights movement, Tometi worked as a caseworker for victims of domestic violence, which further solidified her emerging feminist politics.[23]

Patrisse Khan-Cullors has led campaigns against mass incarceration for years. She began her political activism as a teenager in Los Angeles, where she was influenced by the experiences of her own family. Her dad spent time in and out of California prisons on various drug charges and died in a homeless shelter in 2009. At age twenty, her beloved older brother was wrongfully arrested and thrown into the Los Angeles county jail, where he was beaten unconscious by guards. He was later diagnosed with bipolar disorder. Trying to make sense of how racism and the carceral state had caused so much pain and suffering in her own family, Patrisse turned to political organizing. She began volunteering, first with the LA Bus Riders Union and later with the Labor Strategy Center; both organizations are West Coast centers for multi-issue radical politics and popular education. With an irresistible smile and outgoing personality, Khan-Cullors is the kind of street organizer who inspires people to stop and listen, even when she is talking about a rather somber subject. She went on to lead the Coalition to End Sheriff Violence in Los Angeles and founded the advocacy coalition Dignity and Power Now. In the process she came out as queer and deepened her Black feminist consciousness and commitments.[24]

In this chapter, in truncated fashion, I have attempted to trace some of the political genealogy of BLMM/M4BL—the personal stories of just a handful of its leaders, as well as some of the conditions and circumstances and earlier phases of organizing that laid the groundwork for BLMM/M4BL and made its emergence possible. The strength, determination, and fierce agency of hundreds of dedicated young Black organizers made a possibility into a reality.

TWO

Justice for Trayvon

The Spark

If the police murder of Michael Brown in Ferguson in summer 2014 was the fire that signaled the full-blown emergence of the Black Lives Matter Movement and Movement for Black Lives (BLMM/M4BL), then the vigilante murder with impunity of young Trayvon Martin in Sanford, Florida, in February 2012 was the spark. Trayvon Martin was a Black teenager coming back from buying snacks on a rainy Florida night in the winter of 2012, when he unknowingly stumbled into the path of George Zimmerman. An overly zealous community patrol volunteer, Zimmerman saw a young Black man wearing a hoodie sweatshirt and assumed the worst. In a crude and deadly case of racial profiling, Zimmerman saw Trayvon's skin color and profile and concluded he was up to no good. Ignoring the 911 operator's instructions not to pursue Martin, Zimmerman did so anyway, complaining, "F—king punks ... they always get away."[1] He eventually caught up with Martin and, under circumstances that are still unclear, shot him to death, claiming self-defense. When the story first broke and photos of the handsome, baby-faced Black teenager were circulated on social media, along with the information that he had simply been returning from a trip to a local convenience store to buy candy and a soft drink when he was killed, Black people, especially young Black people, were incensed. Many of them had experienced racial profiling themselves. They identified with Martin. His murder triggered protests in the streets and the formation of several new national or regional organizations, notably Million Hoodies Movement for Justice, Dream Defenders, and Black Youth Project 100.

Weeks after the teenager's murder, as it became increasingly clear that the Florida authorities had no intention of prosecuting his killer, activists called for "Million Hoodies" marches all over the country. The largest march, involving more than five thousand protesters, took place on March 21, 2012, in New York City. There protesters converged on Union Square to hear speeches by Trayvon's parents and others. Similar marches took place in cities across the country, as the hoodie sweatshirt, the item of clothing that Trayvon had been wearing when he was killed, became a political symbol of opposition to racial profiling and the criminalization of Black youth. Celebrities donned hoodies in public gestures of solidarity, and megacelebrities Jay Z and Beyoncé even showed up at one of the New York protests. President Obama expressed sympathy for the parents of Trayvon, reflecting in a public statement that if he had had a son he would have likely resembled Trayvon.[2]

Trayvon's parents, Sybrina Fulton and Tracy Martin, became two of the most compelling voices in the "Justice for Trayvon" campaign, which from the outset extended beyond the boundaries of this single case. "My son is your son," Fulton said repeatedly at rallies and in press conferences. Speakers at the New York rally cited the police shooting of an unarmed Black man,

Ramarley Graham, on February 2, 2012. Invoking Graham and others killed by police connected vigilante violence to state violence. Speakers at the rally also pointed out that the collective anger over Martin's death was not directed simply at a single individual, George Zimmerman, but at the system that failed to prosecute and hold him accountable. Police on the scene, protesters argued, treated Zimmerman as if he were the victim, not Trayvon. Initially, they seemed to accept his version of events without question, even as an unarmed Black boy lay dead.[3] Out of this moment of anger, the Million Hoodies Movement for Justice was founded.

Million Hoodies was the brainchild of digital strategist Daniel Maree, who in March 2012 wrote a blog post and launched a petition calling for the prosecution of Zimmerman. He teamed up with student activists from Howard University and later with Malik Rhassan from Occupy the Hood. Movement strategist Thenjiwe McHarris, who would later cofound Blackbird and would be instrumental in the founding of the Movement for Black Lives Coalition, was also involved at the outset, giving political, tactical, and strategic direction to the effort. Million Hoodies Movement for Justice is a human rights organization led by youth of color devoted to "reimagining safety and justice" for Black and Brown communities. The group has evolved into a not-for-profit, membership-based organization. Its current executive director, Dante Barry, came on board in the summer of 2013, after meeting Maree at the Roosevelt Institute, a liberal think tank. He built up the group's current membership and infrastructure. While the fatal racial profiling of Martin led to the formation of Million Hoodies, the group now works on a range of human rights and racial justice issues and is part of the Freedom Cities network linking racial justice and immigrant rights, working with organizations like the Black Alliance for Just Immigration, the Ella Baker Center for Human Rights, and the immigration rights group Enlace.

Those who were furious when the story of Martin's murder was first reported were even further outraged on July 13, 2013, when George Zimmerman was found not guilty after a highly publicized jury trial. The only reason a trial was held in the first place was that sustained protests in the streets and on social media, along with pressure from Martin's family, forced local officials to reconsider the initial decision not to charge Zimmerman.

The larger political context in which the Martin murder occurred is important. Trayvon Martin was killed four years into Obama's presidency, on the eve of his re-election. The case sparked the largest resurgence of Black protest in over four decades.[4] In light of the lack of recognition of the preponderance of violence against Black people, the Malcolm X Grassroots Movement released a provocative and revealing report in 2013 called "Operation Ghetto Storm," the title borrowed from the US Desert Storm military invasion of Iraq. The well-researched report asserted that a Black person was killed by police, security guards, or vigilantes every twenty-eight hours. This statistic was widely circulated and helped to connect the dots between what authorities argued were isolated incidents of police and related shootings. The *Washington Post* and other mainstream publications questioned the accuracy of the statistic, but as others began to track and document instances of police violence, the presence of a clear pattern and a disturbing uptick of incidents across the country became apparent. The *Post* began to track its own numbers of police shootings, in a documentation project titled "Fatal Force."[5] In a sense, the explosion of protest in the wake of Martin's murder and Zimmerman's acquittal was a quarter century in the making, but more immediately the case underscored the precariousness that defined the lives of Black youth in the United States, especially if they were poor and working class. They were deemed expendable and disposable, activists argued, by a society that had no place for them in a downsized, neoliberal labor market. Black men and boys like Trayvon Martin had already been systemically criminalized, not by their individual actions but by their collective identity, their posture, their positionality, and sometimes even their fashion choices. They were typecast in popular culture and popular media as menacing, violent, and dangerous: bodies to be feared, contained, or even killed.

In the 1990s, future Democratic presidential candidate Hillary Rodham Clinton offered a chilling assessment of a substratum of poor Black urban youth, which came back to haunt her during her 2016 presidential bid, when she was confronted about it by BLMM/M4BL activists. In her words, "They are not just gangs of kids anymore.... They are often the kinds of kids that are called 'super-predators.' No conscience. No empathy. We can talk about why they ended up that way, but first we have to bring them to heel."[6] While she did not mention race or blackness explicitly, and nearly twenty years later expressed regret at having made the statement, the implication was clear. These labels effectively vilified and socially disenfranchised a whole generation of poor and working-class Black youth.

While there is a particular aspect of this narrative that stereotypes young Black men and boys as potentially violent criminals deserving of cages and condemnation, there is a parallel set of stereotypes that has been applied to young Black women and girls, portraying them as irresponsible and sexually promiscuous. In the 1980s, Ronald Reagan used the term *welfare queen* to malign poor women and typecast poor Black single mothers as undeserving of government aid. This vilification was part of a neoliberal narrative that created a racialized profile of an undeserving "underclass," as a precursor to, companion of, and pretext for the dismantling of the welfare system. This was a blow, not only to the black poor, but to all poor people in the United States, that was propagated under the false assumption that welfare programs were racial subsidies for the Black poor. These dual stereotypes reduced Black boys and girls and young adults to pathologized caricatures.

The Florida-based Dream Defenders, a multiracial group led by Black, Latinx, immigrant, and Palestinian young people, was the first major group in the South to emerge in the wake of Martin's murder in 2012. Dream Defenders' organizers rejected the racist stereotypes that dehumanize Black youth and were infuriated by the wanton killing of Trayvon Martin. The organization was founded by Phillip Agnew (known for two years as Umi Selah), Ahmad Abuznaid, Gabriel Pendas, Ciara Taylor, Nelini Stamp, Michael Sampson, Nailah Summers, and the forty young organizers who participated in the group's first march.[7] Key organizers who helped shape the group early on include Curtis Hierro, Jonel Edwards, Steven Pargett, Eli Armstrong, Sandra Khalifa, and Sherika Shaw.

In 2006, Agnew, Abuznaid, and Pendas formed the Student Coalition for Justice in response to the killing of Florida teenager Martin Lee Anderson at a state juvenile detention facility. For three days, they organized students on the campuses of Florida A&M University, Florida State University, and Tallahassee Community College to occupy Governor Jeb Bush's office and to hold demonstrations. Their actions forced Bush to call for an in-depth investigation into Anderson's murder.

When Trayvon Martin was killed in 2012, many Black Florida activists felt compelled again to take action. Channeling historic long marches, Dream Defenders organized sixty students to make a forty-mile trek from Bethune Cookman College in Daytona Beach to Sanford, Florida, to draw attention to the forty days after Martin's death during which George Zimmerman was not charged with his murder. He was arrested a few days later. Their most high-profile direct action was launched the following year, three days after Zimmerman's "not guilty" verdict was announced, when hundreds of protesters embarked on a month-long occupation of the Florida governor's office. Ultimately, they did not achieve their immediate goal, which was to force the passage of Trayvon's Law, a slate of legislative bills that sought to address racial profiling and Florida's biased "Stand Your Ground" law. However, they did advance their agenda to bring attention to "the school-to-prison pipeline" and the criminalization of Black and Brown youth. They also upped their profile and membership, which prepared them for the fights that lay ahead.

Even though mainstream media often gravitated to the charismatic Agnew, women who had significant experience were also instrumental in the political development and organizational evolution of Dream Defenders. For example, Ciara Taylor served as the group's political director, having been an organizer with other progressive groups, including the American Civil Liberties Union and Southern Poverty Law Center. Nelini Stamp, who was a core leader during Occupy Wall Street in New York City, began organizing with Working Families Party in 2008. Summers and Khalifa, alongside Pargett, molded the communications and cultural strategy of the organization, finding new and innovative ways to reach young Black people.

Local organizers Jonel Edwards and Sherika Shaw helped expand the organization's membership base by supporting the recruitment and development of new chapters. They also founded the organization's high school programs. In addition, Shaw launched the organization's Womyn's Faction, a leadership development program aimed at supporting and elevating women's leadership in the organization.[8]

Rachel Gilmer joined the organization in 2015 as the chief of strategy (she would later become codirector alongside Agnew), after working with Black feminist legal scholar Kimberlé Crenshaw at the African American Policy Forum. A grassroots organizer, who had been part of community-based and youth organizing campaigns and programs in New York State and Portland, Oregon, Gilmer was brought on to help the organization hone its strategic focus after nearly three years of fighting. She has been an intellectual and political force within the organization alongside Agnew ever since. Dream Defenders became her political home.

As chief of strategy, Gilmer oversaw the group's input into the historic "Vision for Black Lives" statement. Her contribution was to underscore the importance of the international context and to highlight one of the most controversial issues in the document—its recognition of the suffering, rights, and aspirations of the Palestinian people. In her words, after participating in a delegation to occupied Palestine, she insisted, "We are never going to get free in the U.S. if the rest of the world is in chains."[9]

Gilmer's history is an interesting one. In the 1990s, her parents, who had their own share of personal challenges, left San Francisco to live communally in an experimental community in Oregon. The family eventually migrated to Mississippi, and then back to Oregon. Along the way, Rachel, whose mother is white and whose father is Black, wrestled with issues of color, racism, white supremacy, and her own personal traumas. As a student at Vassar, she recalls, "The universe introduced me to James Baldwin ... and my life changed forever."[10]

In its founding statement, Dream Defenders describes its membership as "products of a Dream Deferred, witnesses to a Dream damaged and destroyed," a nod to both Dr. Martin Luther King's famous "I Have a Dream" speech and Langston Hughes's seminal poem, in which the poet threatens an "explosion" if the dreams of the oppressed and downtrodden are not realized.[11] Dream Defenders is also decidedly local and regional, with nearly a dozen chapters (which they refer to as squadds—the extra *d* being for Dream Defenders) throughout the state of Florida. However, the impact and reach of the group has been both national and international. Cofounder Abuznaid coordinated a delegation to Palestine that included Charlene Carruthers, Patrisse Khan-Cullors, Tef Poe, Phillip Agnew, Rachel Gilmer, and others.[12] The delegation visited schools and refugee camps and met with Palestinian youth. Since then, they have organized two more delegations, which have been eye-opening and life-altering experiences for participants. Scholar-activist Maytha Alhassen was also instrumental in organizing the Black and people of color delegations to Palestine around this time.

Over time, a Black feminist praxis has come to inform the work of this group as well. The first sentence of its seven-point vision statement reads, "We believe that our liberation necessitates the destruction of the political and economic systems of Capitalism and Imperialism as well as Patriarchy."[13] Like other BLMM/M4BL groups, Dream Defenders has set up mechanisms to deal with internal issues of sexism, homophobia, and harmful behavior within the group: a system of accountability.

Members have been suspended from the group after allegations of sexual harassment surfaced and were verified.[14]

Another group that came out of the crucible moment of the Martin murder and the Zimmerman acquittal was BYP100. This is how it began. Black feminist and queer activist Cathy Cohen, a senior political science professor at the University of Chicago, launched a research project in 2005–2006 to document, analyze, and amplify the often-ignored voices of young Black people. Inspired by her research findings, she decided to organize a national convening of young Black leaders from across the country to see what kind of activist projects might be incubated. As she writes in her book *Democracy Remixed,* Cohen's motivation was not purely academic. The daughter of Black working-class parents from Toledo, she had seen firsthand the effects of racism and marginalization on Black youth. Her nephew had been pushed out of school, had been caught up in the underground economy in Ohio, and ended up in prison. It was the voice of young people like him she felt needed to be heard. Cohen recognized there was much being said about Black youth in media and scholarship, but very few were asking Black millennials what they themselves thought, believed, and felt.

With the help of a part-time assistant and local Chicago organizers, and with the input of a youth advisory council, Cohen identified an eclectic cohort of activists from across the country and invited them to Chicago. Under the "Beyond November Movement" rubric, a reference to the November 2012 presidential election, roughly a hundred Black youth leaders (ages 18–35) met in a suburb outside Chicago in July 2013. Some of those convened knew one another through informal activist and social circles, but they did not know what this gathering would lead to. Some were admittedly skeptical.[15] The goal was to explore organizational possibilities, but no one could have predicted that things would unfold precisely as they did.

Some attendees were college students and college graduates, but many were not. One vocal and influential member of the original group had a partner who was incarcerated at the time. Another participant was a survivor of Illinois's notoriously racist foster care system. Others had grown up in low-income neighborhoods and housing projects from New York to St. Louis to Detroit. There were also some among them who attended private schools and elite colleges and worked for prominent nonprofit organizations. It was a diverse cross section. Many of them identified as queer or gender nonconforming. Overall, the BYP100 founders represented the breadth of the Black millennial experience. Most notably, they included those who had experienced firsthand the blunt traumas of US racial capitalism and hetero-patriarchy.

The conclusion of the Zimmerman trial coincided with the inaugural meeting of the Beyond November group. By the time it was announced that the jury had reached a verdict, the meeting had already adjourned, but the attendees reconvened, held hands, and waited to hear the news. The timing of the not guilty verdict was fortuitous. Some of the young people cried, and others were stoic. "It was a moment of trauma and a moment of clarity," Carruthers later reflected.[16] The announcement struck a chord. Social media was on fire, and so were the people who were about to form this historic new organization. Half the group hunkered down in the spirit of what Dr. King called "the fierce urgency of now," hammering out the language of a statement that would condemn the verdict. Another contingent leapt into action and began what would be the steady stream of BYP100's direct action work. Some drove, and others piled on the train to downtown Chicago to participate in marches and vigils with people from across the city.

The neophyte group found themselves leading those protests. While they cried and chanted, in both belief and disbelief at the verdict, some of them remember that evening as a moment that propelled them into full-time political activism.

In August 2013, on the eve of the fiftieth anniversary of the historic March on Washington, a core of young activists from the "Beyond November" meeting gathered at the headquarters of the Human Rights Campaign (HRC) in Washington, DC, not because they were in sync politically with HRC, but because the space was offered. There, they hammered out what became BYP100's founding documents, mission statement, and core values. Cohen was also on hand for that historic DC meeting and march. BYP100 launched its organizing and political education work in 2013 and steadily expanded and intensified that work over the months and years that followed.

A native of Chicago's South Side, Carruthers had several years of organizing to her credit. "Unapologetically black" and unapologetically queer at age twenty-seven, she accepted a position as the group's dynamic new national coordinator in 2013. The job title has evolved. Carruthers is now the national director of BYP100. Whatever her title, this job is important to her. After working in several white-led and male-led organizations, the confident young organizer can finally put her intersectional feminist politics to work empowering Black millennials.[17]

BYP100's initial funding was made possible by Cohen's membership on the board of the Arcus Foundation, a family foundation run by philanthropist Jon Stryker that focuses on, among other things, supporting LGBTQIA issues and leadership.[18] Cohen made the case to the board that it should take a chance and lend resources to the new formation, because Black youth organizing, informed by Black feminist and queer politics, is what LGBTQIA funders ought to be supporting. That investment allowed BYP100 to hire staff, obtain space, and convene meetings for the first few years of its existence.

In addition to Carruthers, founding members included spoken word poet Malcolm London, District of Columbia voter rights organizer Jessica Pierce (one of the two initial cochairs), Chicago organizer Charity Tolliver, Chicago native Aisha Truss-Miller, and nineteen-year-old college student Asha Ransby-Sporn. Those attending the meeting that led to BYP100's formation also included Jonathan Lykes, a queer artist and student activist whose work centers around promoting Black Joy for survival and resistance; Chris Buford, a Chicago youth organizer who helped lead the fight against the conditions in the Audy Home, Chicago's juvenile detention center; Karess Taylor-Hughes, who had worked on the national marriage equality campaign; Jazz Hudson, an artist and educator from Oakland; as well as Terrance Laney and Rose Afriyie, to name only a few of the hundred.

Cohen had a fragile faith in the new formation. Others, including myself, thought they needed, for lack of a better term, more "adult supervision." "Don't they need gentle guidance?" I prodded my dear friend. But Cathy, a woman of unmistakably strong views, took a decidedly gentler approach. She spoke her mind, to be sure; helped them secure much-needed resources; met with them; and offered advice, but she was, in true Ella Baker fashion, determined that the organization be theirs. Even if the members made a misstep or two, they would be their missteps, not ours. She was right. BYP100 engaged in a year of meetings, trainings, retreats, and recruitment, and when the Ferguson protests exploded in summer 2014, they were ready to respond and support the uprising. Many BYP100 members took supplies to Ferguson and participated in the street demonstrations. They were deeply impacted by their experiences, which included suffering teargas, witnessing violent arrests, and facing down heavily armed police. On returning to their home cities, they were fortified and intent upon building a movement.[19] In the year after BYP100's founding, new members engaged in two major actions. One was to protest, along with other groups, the national convention of ALEC (The American Legislative Exchange Council), a secretive and highly influential conservative think tank that develops "model policies for legislators," including the racist "Stand Your Ground" laws around the country. The second action was the takeover of the Florida State Capitol. BYP100 members, including Charlene Carruthers, went to Florida to support the Dream Defenders' action there. They were getting their feet wet in new political waters.

BYP100 quickly became a magnet for Black youth looking for an outlet for their political passions and a community with which to struggle, grow, and build. Although chapters in other cities were formed in 2013, Chicago became the hub. And it was fertile ground to grow a new organization. Chicago has a long and rich history of political struggle and holds a special place in the history of the Black Freedom Movement in the United States. In 2013, powerful young Chicago activists, who were steeped in that tradition, formed the backbone of BYP100.

In addition to those already mentioned, BYP100's Chicago-based organizers included Johnáe Strong, Breanna Champion, Valerie Papillon, and Rachel Williams. Key members like Maxx Boykin and Todd St. Hill came aboard later. Asha Ransby-Sporn and Brianna Gibson, who had gained collective organizing experience in Chicago, New York, and Oakland, were later hired as national organizing cochairs. Asha had helped to build the New York City chapter as a student at Columbia while also participating in Students against Mass Incarceration (SAMI). Brianna had previously worked with a BLM chapter in Oakland. As of this writing, they travel the country helping to bolster new chapters and jumpstart campaigns. After her leadership roles in BYP100's Chicago chapter and antiviolence organizing work, Janae Bonsu, a social work graduate student, became the group's national public policy chair and oversaw the publication of one of BYP100's first policy documents, "Agenda to Build Black Futures," which centers on economic justice. Like a number of other BYP100 members whose families come from the African Diaspora beyond the United States, Janae's father's family is from Ghana, which informs her global view of Black politics. She continues to play a prominent role.

Jasson Perez (the other national cochair), a thirty-something Afro–Puerto Rican activist and self-taught social and economic theorist, was an important anchor for the Chicago group and the growing national body during its first two years. An avid reader, former rapper (with a group sarcastically named BBU—Black, Brown, and Ugly), single dad, and former union organizer, Jasson served as mentor and youthful griot to the cadre of even younger organizers. His penchant for theorizing and Carruthers's brilliance as a strategist made them a powerful team for the first two years of BYP100's existence.

Another local Chicago leader was Angie Rollins, otherwise known as Fresco Steez (later tapped to serve as BYP100's national digital strategist). A sensitive but tough-talking young Black, queer organizer from Chicago's South Side, she had already spent a good part of her teen years as a community organizer. She first participated in leadership training and political education with a nonprofit called the Southwest Youth Collaborative, which was run at the time by Palestinian activist and beloved Chicago organizer Camille Odeh. Fresco had also worked with

Fearless Leading by the Youth, had led youth delegations to Haiti, and was tied into a larger network of the city's Black youth organizers. Fresco was just the kind of sharp-edged and committed organizer that BYP100 needed and wanted. She was dynamite on a bullhorn and no pushover in contentious meetings. Later she became instrumental in building the Washington, DC, chapter of the organization.

Not all of BYP100's members are queer, but the group defines itself explicitly as operating through a "Black queer feminist lens." This approach, inspired by the intellectual midwifery of Cohen and other Black feminists, is reflected in who leads the group, what issues they take up, and how they carry out and frame the work. There is an insistence, for example, on including cis and trans women, and queer and trans victims of police violence, in their campaigns, even though the predominant image of those harmed by police in mainstream accounts is cisgender males.[20]

While the acquittal of Trayvon Martin's killer dominated the headlines and captured the attention of most Black organizers in 2012–13, the case of Marissa Alexander, also in Florida, brought the gender politics of state violence front and center. Although a small cohort of activists rallied around Alexander early on, most Black feminist organizers became aware of the case around the same time the Zimmerman trial was getting under way. Her saga had begun years earlier. The contrast was stark. Alexander was a survivor of domestic violence who had been jailed for daring to defend herself and her children against her estranged husband. She had fired a warning shot with her licensed gun, which lodged in the ceiling of her home, to prevent her husband from harming her. No one was hurt. Like Zimmerman, she claimed she acted in self-defense, but the authorities were not sympathetic and the mainstream media virtually ignored her case.

When the fateful incident occurred in 2010, Alexander, a mother of three, had just nine days earlier given birth to her third child. Still, she was tried, convicted after a twelve-minute jury deliberation, and sentenced to an outrageous term of twenty years in prison for her actions. She was not afforded the benefit of Florida's controversial Stand Your Ground law, which supposedly allows for gun use in self-defense.

A Black-led group of feminist antiviolence organizers and lawyers, and one antiracist white activist, heard about the case and came to Alexander's defense, forming the coalition "Free Marissa Now." In a decentralized but coordinated fashion, the coalition fundraised tens of thousands of dollars for Marissa's legal defense; hosted teach-ins, vigils, and letter-writing efforts; and even enlisted artists to design posters and T-shirts to spread the word. Free Marissa Now, developed as an alliance of organizations and activists, involved groups in Chicago, Phoenix, Jacksonville, Seattle, Pittsburgh, and Oakland. The core organizing team included members from the African-American/Black Women's Cultural Alliance, the New Jim Crow Movement, and INCITE! Local groups like Project NIA, led by Black feminist powerhouse Mariame Kaba, helped launch a Chicago-based defense committee to support Marissa; at the same time, in St. Louis, Sistahs Talkin' Back fundraised to support Marissa's freedom. This case, which prosecutors had viewed as closed, was reopened, essentially by the sheer willpower of the women activists and male supporters who embraced Alexander's plight with formidable resolve. While organizers made Alexander's freedom their priority, they also used the case to expose the unfair treatment of Black women, especially Black mothers, in the courts and prison system.[21]

The feminist women of color–led group SisterSong, based in Atlanta, Georgia, also lent its energies and leadership to the campaign. The members partnered with the Free Marissa Campaign in the summer of 2014 to host a week of action in Florida entitled "Standing Our Ground: Raising Our Voices against Reproductive Oppression, Gender Violence and Mass Incarceration," in which hundreds of people participated. SisterSong's involvement was important in offering a reproductive justice framework to the politics of Alexander's case.[22]

Alexander's case dragged on long after George Zimmerman's acquittal. Ultimately she opted to end the ordeal and agreed to a plea bargain. Her twenty-year sentence was overturned but not her conviction. She ended up spending a total of three years in jail and prison; in January 2015, she was released after agreeing to accept house arrest, including ankle monitor surveillance, for up to two more years.[23] Although the victory was a partial one, the Free Marissa Now Campaign exposed the many ways Black women are criminalized and set the tone for the campaigns to follow.

The mobilization around Marissa Alexander's case was an early indication that this phase of the Black Freedom Movement was not going to be male-centered but would be informed by Black feminist politics. Even before the explosion of protests in 2014, the narrative of the gendered nature of state violence with respect to the African American community, and the leadership that would frame the most brazen response to it, had shifted.

THREE

The Ferguson Uprising and Its Reverberations

Michael Brown, an unarmed eighteen-year-old Black youth, was shot dead by police officer Darren Wilson on August 9, 2014, on the streets of Ferguson, Missouri. His body was left in the street for hours. That simple horrific incident, and the sustained protests that followed, would change lives, attitudes, careers, and the direction of Black politics in the United States.

Walking down the street with a friend hours after a minor altercation at a local convenience store, Michael Brown was not in the mood to be told what to do. And the white cop who stopped him, Darren Wilson, riding alone in a patrol car, was not in the mood to have his orders disobeyed. Wilson told Brown and his friend Dorian Johnson not to walk in the street. They talked back to him, telling Wilson they were almost at their destination and would be on the sidewalk soon enough. At that point, they were just two young Black men, who presumably, in the mind of the officer, needed to be "checked." He then allegedly realized that Brown fit the description of a person involved in a shoving and shoplifting incident at a local convenience store; things escalated from there.[1]

Wilson later testified that Brown "looked like a demon" on the day the confrontation and killing occurred. In other words, he was not afforded the status of human—not because of what he had done but because of who he *was*. He was not just a husky teenager with a cocky attitude. He was not a kid who loved video games or had struggled in high school; he was not a son whose mother had struggled to put food on the table and was planning to go to college.[2] He was not an unarmed local kid simply refusing to follow instructions. He was a "demon." Wilson's view, as it turns out, was not so inconsistent with that of other white Ferguson police officers regarding local Black youth, as demonstrated in a damning Department of Justice report that documented a pattern of consistent racial profiling, harassment, and strong-arm tactics by the Ferguson police.[3]

There was no videotape of Brown's murder, and the victim obviously could not tell his side of the story. Darren Wilson described an implausible set of events that conveniently absolved him of any wrongdoing in this case. According to him, he simply told Brown and his friend to walk on the sidewalk, not in the street. They refused, and a heated exchange ensued. Brown allegedly reached into the police car (knowing full well that Wilson was armed), threatened Wilson, and "forced" him to fatally shoot the teen. Any reasonable person would question the veracity of such an account. What is uncontested, however, is that at the end of a brief exchange, an unarmed young Black teenager was dead in the street. What happened next probably triggered rebellion as much as the shooting itself. Michael Brown's lifeless body was left in the middle of Canfield Avenue as crowds gathered and news of the latest murder spread by cell phone, texts, and Twitter. This callous disregard for Brown's basic humanity had "Black Lives DON'T Matter" written all over it.

Ferguson's Black community was outraged at Brown's murder. I tell the story of Brown talking back to Darren Wilson, and the alleged convenience store incident, to make a point. By all indications, Michael Brown was not a saint. However, in the resistance that followed his death, organizers insisted he did not have to be. There did not have to be a correlation between "sainthood" and Black citizenship. This was an important shift in the discourse about who is or is not a sympathetic victim of injustice. Brown did not have to be a church-going, law-abiding, proper-speaking embodiment of respectability in order for his life to matter, protesters insisted. And they insisted loudly.

After the shooting, neighbors initially stood around in disgust, witnessing the grizzly spectacle and demanding answers. After the body was removed, protests and vigils sprang up spontaneously. A memorial with flowers, photos, and stuffed animals was first set up at the site of the shooting. A police car reportedly drove over the makeshift memorial and destroyed it, which many saw as another gesture of callous disregard for Black suffering and mourning. The second night, hundreds of Ferguson residents poured into the streets. They marched, chanted, sang, and refused to disperse when police demanded that they do so. They were fed up. This would not be just another routine police murder. Not this time. What had been routine would become unacceptable.

Many chants reverberated throughout the Ferguson uprising, including "Hands Up, Don't Shoot," which evoked reports that Brown was in a surrendering posture when he was gunned down. However, it is the powerful and far-reaching slogan "Black lives matter" that finally took hold as the rubric under which a larger movement would ultimately rally. Some have argued that the term was imposed upon the movement by media, who latched onto it. But whatever propelled it into the public square, it struck a chord with Black people and others. Understanding that the systemic criminalization and devaluation of Black life is part of the current regime of racial capitalism is crucial to understanding Brown's murder and why "Black lives matter" as a slogan has had such a deep resonance. It is a counternarrative to the barrage of messages that insist the lives of the Black urban poor do *not* matter.[4]

Scholar and journalist Marc Lamont Hill makes the compelling and provocative assertion that the Michael Browns of the world have been relegated by the state and dominant society to the status of "nobody." In his words, "To be Nobody is to be considered disposable.... Underneath each case (of state violence) is a more fundamental set of economic conditions, political arrangements, and power relations that transform everyday citizens into casualties of an increasingly intense war on the vulnerable."[5] He cites underfunded schools, lack of access to affordable housing and jobs, as well as heavy-handed policing and a behemoth prison industry as some of the weapons amassed against young Black men like Brown, who have become "excesses" to the current formal economy. The Ferguson uprising insisted that Michael Brown was indeed "somebody."

At the outset, the Ferguson protests included an assortment of forces: religious leaders held candles and knelt in prayer; Black civic leaders and elected officials from St. Louis, like Antonio French, who became ubiquitous on Twitter and CNN, gave speeches and interviews. But there was another group that took to the streets and held the streets. It was their bold actions that engendered the slogan "Whose Streets? Our Streets," also the title of a powerful 2017 documentary about Ferguson. They were angry and fed-up Black youth—Michael Brown's peers—who were tired of being harassed by the local white police force. They were young people who would eventually read the whole system of injustice into Brown's untimely death, and disrespected corpse. Some protested peacefully but defiantly, while a small number took out their anger on parked cars and, eventually, on local businesses. There was looting. Windows were smashed, cars and trashcans were torched, and a few cars were overturned in the course of the uprising. However, for the most part protests were both militant and nonviolent at the same time.

The bottom line was that in a few short days, after a series of incendiary actions by local authorities, Ferguson's Black population had become ungovernable. Those who sought to govern had lost all credibility with a key sector of the population. Local police had little influence on the crowds, and curfews were ignored. On August 18, Missouri governor Jay Nixon called in the National Guard, which only added to the tensions.

From the very beginning, a key factor fueling the historic Ferguson rebellion was the hyperbolic and militaristic response of the local and state authorities. Ferguson's police officers (and St. Louis–area backup teams) showed up heavily armed with combat weapons and tanks—surplus from the US military.[6] Local cops took a hostile approach from the start. There were numerous accounts of cops taunting the protesters, rough-handling reporters, and using a level of force seemingly designed to be provocative.[7]

One local person who became a prominent leader in the streets of Ferguson that summer and fall was Brittany Ferrell, a young nursing student with a six-year-old daughter. She impacted the struggle, and the struggle profoundly impacted her. Ferrell had been active on her college campus before August 2014, but nothing prepared her for the uprising. Brittany, having heard about the shooting on social media and feeling she had to do something, returned home early from vacation to see what was going on. She remembers having a conversation with her young daughter to try to explain the grim reality before they went out to join protesters in the street. That was day 2. From that point on she was drawn into the protest and became one of its most formidable voices. She was out there every day for weeks, lost her job, and found an exhilarating sense of purpose and community; at the same time, she experienced a lot of outright "cruelty," in her words, in the form of sexist and homophobic remarks from a small but vocal group of fellow protesters: "It was as if because my body was unavailable [to men] I was out of my place or I was trying to emasculate Black men."[8] Nevertheless, she persevered, with these experiences fueling her feminist sensibilities as well as her determination to continue resisting racist police violence toward all Black people.[9]

Ferrell went from a neophyte protester motivated by a visceral anger at injustices she had witnessed her whole life to a savvy, and seemingly fearless, organizer. Along the way, she participated in meetings and strategy sessions and helped organize workshops on women's leadership. She honed her public-speaking and chant-leading skills. She sought advice from those with more experience. "I would never downplay the knowledge that Merv [Marcano from Blackbird], Patrisse [Khan-Cullors], and Alicia [Garza] brought to the situation," she reflected. "They brought wisdom from their experience and from elders."[10] She sought out advice from Garza in particular, and her counsel was helpful. In addition to acknowledging those who came from elsewhere, Ferrell remembers and recognizes that she was inspired by those local people whose names never made it into the newspaper: Tony Rice, Ebony Williams, Derek Robinson, Diamond Latchison, and Low-Key from Lost Voices, who was only fifteen when the protests began.[11]

Kayla Reed is another St. Louis–area local whose life was changed by the murder of Michael Brown that fateful summer day in August 2014. After she finished her shift as a pharmacy technician, her "cracked and crappy" Samsung phone was lighting up with texts about what had just happened in Ferguson.[12] She picked up her friend Tef Poe, and they were out on the streets the first night to participate in the protests, not knowing how long they would be sustained. "I went to sleep that night thinking it was over," she recalled, "but I woke up and it wasn't."[13] That recognition became a pivot point for Kayla and sent her life in directions she had not foreseen. She, like so many others, was enraged by the heavy-handed tactics of the police and inspired by the courage of her fellow protesters.

Kayla keenly observed the dialectics of struggle in Ferguson. There was, on the one hand, a great sense of camaraderie and community building. On the other hand, there were tensions, fissures, and even budding hostilities between different sectors of the embryonic movement and between different personalities. Kayla spent a lot of time at a local apartment where Ferguson protesters crashed. Some called it a "safe house," where people could eat, sleep, and refuel before returning to the streets. She remembers getting up every morning and cooking dozens of eggs and two pounds of bacon and potatoes for her new political family. That was an important period of bonding for the newly constituted activist community.

But among the local protesters, there were stresses—about money, tactics, and who could or should speak for the movement. And when supporters came from out of state, some locals reacted with a mixture of skepticism and gratitude. Kayla remembered that when she first met social media personality

DeRay Mckesson, who had just arrived from Baltimore, she cursed him out because she was "trying to tell people to do one thing" and he was trying to tell her to do something else. They later became friends.[14]

Kayla, a confident, savvy young woman with a magnetic personality, is overall grateful to the movement for many things. "It's not lost on me for one day that when this thing began I was a pharmacy tech, ... and a lot of people invested in me" to develop her leadership skills. But there is something else profoundly personal. Kayla, the daughter and granddaughter of preachers, came out as queer after her involvement in the movement and is now happily partnered with a fellow activist. In reflecting on that process, she says, "The movement affirmed a part of me that I was not affirming for twenty-five years."[15] Her coming-out story illustrates the ways in which personal transformation and political transformation are, for many, bound together.

Personal stories like Kayla's and Brittany's played out against the larger backdrop of Ferguson, a town whose combined history, politics, and dominant culture created fertile soil to grow Black protest. Ferguson, Missouri, had an abusive, virtually all-white police force that had essentially occupied and ridden roughshod over the Black population of this little town for years. They were no doubt unsettled by the fact that Black residents were finally rising up against the tyranny that had become routine.[16]

The Ferguson uprising was a moment that reenergized veteran St. Louis activists like sixty-plus-year-old Jamala Rogers of the Organization for Black Struggle, who is lovingly referred to as "Mama Jamala" by younger activists and was one of the leaders and the first staff person of the Black Radical Congress. Rogers's sage wisdom and firm but loving advice were enormous assets to the young activists who took to the streets in Ferguson. She was often the first person people called when they arrived in town to help, or when they encountered a problem or dilemma locally. Montague Simmons, the executive director of the Organization for Black Struggle (OBS), was also an indispensable human resource and anchor for the protesters, spending many hours in meetings, marches, and direct-action training sessions. A St. Louis native, Simmons took Brown's death personally. When asked by journalist Jamilah Lemieux what he would say to the late Mike Brown if he could, an emotional Simmons replied, "I wish we'd been in the streets before August 9th. I feel like I failed Mike Brown, because I walked the same streets he did. I went to the same high school, the same junior high, and dealt with the same persecution before it ever touched him. And I fault myself for not finding ways to resist more thoroughly, for not agitating other folks' ambition to resist in light of these systems before it got to him."[17] In addition to reenergizing seasoned organizers like Rogers and Simmons, the Ferguson protests also produced a cadre of new protesters, many of whom went on to become full-fledged organizers. Their experiences of personal and political transformation are important and telling. While high-profile activists have emerged from Ferguson, and from the Black Lives Matter Movement and Movement for Black Lives (BLMM/M4BL) in general, and have gained new levels of celebrity, most have labored in relative obscurity. It is the latter group whose stories are in some ways most revealing.

Ferguson activist Rasheed Aldridge, a small, slender young man who walks with a slight limp, grew up in St. Louis and was working at a car rental agency at the St. Louis airport when the Brown murder occurred. He had met his friend Janina, whom he considers to be like a sister, in the "Fight for 15" movement to increase the minimum wage. She worked at the McDonald's in Ferguson and was one of the first people he called when the news of Brown's murder blew up on Twitter. He got involved on day 2, telling Janina, "We need to take the skills we learned from the Fight for 15 [and try to help]."[18] He said they quickly discovered the situation was too volatile and "organic" for more traditional modes of organizing. Still, he threw himself into the protests and was rewarded with new lessons and an expanded political community.

"I did not know those people from a can of paint when I first went out there, except my friend Janina, but we bonded and we tried to keep each other safe and protect each other"—for example, using Maalox and milk to ease the sting of teargas, aiding strangers who had, in the moment of standing on the barricades together, become their allies.[19] This was in spite of, and alongside of, very real political and tactical differences among the protesters that were reflected in the slogans, actions, language, and sensibilities of the large amorphous crowd. Aldridge eventually left his job to become a full-time organizer. He was the youngest member of the Ferguson Commission, a body established by Missouri's governor to assess the grievances that gave rise to the protests. He was also part of the delegation that visited the White House in December 2014 to meet with President Obama and his staff about the implications of Ferguson for the nation.

Nabeegah Azeri was working as a probation/parole officer, trying, in her own words, to "change the system from within" when the Ferguson uprising occurred. A friend from her Islamic Center recruited her to hand out water bottles to protesters. This began as an innocent and somewhat naïve gesture of support. "I didn't know what else to do"—she confessed that this marked the beginning of her politicization. She got pulled into a peaceful march on day 7 of the protest, but when she and her friend's eight-year-old son quickly encountered tanks and heavily armed police,

she realized she was in the midst of something she had not anticipated. She began going to mass meetings, joined the jail support
team, and launched herself into the uprising. She attended actions
almost every night. A few months later, she quit her job and began
working as a full-time paid staff person at the local nonprofit
MORE (Missourians Organizing for Reform and Empowerment).
For Azeri and many others whom I interviewed, the Ferguson
uprising intensified their political awareness and propelled them
into a long-term commitment to the fight for racial and social
justice.

Two non-Black, St. Louis–area women organizers who were
also deeply involved in the Ferguson protest movement were
Elizabeth Vega, a fifty-plus-year-old Chicana mother, who put
her life on hold to join the protests and mobilizations after
Michael Brown's death, and Julia Ho, a twenty-three-year-old
Asian American former student and environmental activist, who
was working for a local nonprofit when the events of August 9,
2014, occurred. Elizabeth suffered arrest and harassment, lost her
car, and endured many sleepless nights, but she considered enduring these things worth it to stand up to intolerable injustice. Julia
helped to coordinate the essential "bail fund" for the hundreds of
Ferguson protestors who were arrested over the course of the
uprising.[20] They were two among many. Vega also worked with a
small group of local artists, including Damon Davis, to construct
a piece of performance art that was showcased during "Ferguson
October" (a large-scale resistance campaign). It was a wooden coffin with mirrored panels affixed to it on all six sides. *Mirror Casket*
was carried through the streets of Ferguson during the protests to
symbolize Brown's death but also to have both protesters and
police see their faces reflected in the mirrors. His death and their
actions were entangled in the imagery that was produced. The

Smithsonian's National Museum of African American History and Culture acquired the coffin, which is part of its collection of Black protest artifacts.[21]

All kinds of people took to the streets of Ferguson during the height of the protests, but as one organizer observed, at the end of the day "it was mostly poor people, poor Black people, who held it down the longest."[22] One such group, which became an important part of the Ferguson movement ecosystem, named themselves "Lost Voices." These were local Black youth who literally set up camp on the streets of Ferguson after Brown's murder. There is something about a physical occupation of public space that manifests the urgency of the moment. The encampment of a few dozen youth, all with a steel-willed determination to be visible symbols of resistance, evolved into a center for tactical debates, political education, trust building, and protest planning. The members of Lost Voices became mainstays in the nightly street protests.[23]

Two other important local groups that emerged out of Ferguson were Hands Up United and Millennial Activists United (MAU). Hands Up United was built largely by poet-activist and community-based intellectual Tef Poe and a cohort of St. Louis activists. The group describes itself as "a collective of politically engaged minds building towards the liberation of oppressed Black, Brown and poor people through education, art, civil disobedience and agriculture."[24] Hands Up United emphasizes the connection between race and class politics, pledging to counter "attacks on the poor" and "reclaim the war on hunger."[25] Hands Up United's signature program is its Books and Breakfast gatherings, which are reminiscent of the Black Panther Party's free breakfast programs. A meal is served in advance of a hearty political education session or film screening. The Books and Breakfast program has been replicated in a number of cities outside St. Louis.

Three of the four founders of MAU were Black queer women, who like many others were new to activism. They included Brittany Ferrell and Alexis Templeton, who in 2014 were twenty-five and twenty, respectively. They are now married to each other. The other cofounders were Ashley Yates and Larry Fellows III.[26] Templeton speaks openly about her own personal trauma before the Ferguson uprising. Having lost her family in a tragic car accident a short time before the uprising, she found meaning and hope in struggle. Speaking at the 2015 LGBTQIA activists' annual "Creating Change" conference in Denver, Templeton confessed that after struggling with depression and multiple suicide attempts, "Mike Brown saved my life. I was able to put my struggle in this bullhorn."[27] MAU made it clear from the outset that they were about fighting sexism as well as racism. Ferrell commented in an interview with *Nylon* magazine, and reiterated in an interview with the author, that "racism and patriarchy go hand in hand."[28] Feminist views and sensibilities like Ferrell's percolated throughout the Ferguson protests and the national movement as it took off.

When I suggest that the movement is a Black feminist–led movement, I am not naively asserting that there was no opposition and contestation over leadership, or that everyone involved subscribed to feminist views. Nevertheless, when we listen carefully, we realize that the most coherent, consistent, and resolute political voices to emerge over the years since 2012 have been Black feminist voices, or Black feminist–influenced voices.

Darnell Moore, who spent time on the streets of Ferguson, co-coordinated the solidarity freedom ride that helped to launch the Black Lives Matter Global Network (BLMGN), and interviewed the leaders of MAU for *The Feminist Wire*, writes, "Not all of the freedom fighters are Black men with masculine swag and pedigree. Not all of them are cisgender and straight and able-bodied.

Some of us are women. Some of us are queer. Some of us are trans. Some of us are poor. Some of us are disabled. And, yet, all of us desire the same: an end to anti-black policies, practices, and ideologies."[29] These are the kinds of intersectional feminist politics that were injected into the protests in Ferguson.

Another set of political actors on the streets of Ferguson in the summer and fall of 2014 were local faith-based civil rights groups that joined forces to form the broad-based Don't Shoot Coalition. In a different time, the local male clergy would have been in the forefront. But this time was different. Ferguson marked a pivotal turning point in the late twentieth- and twenty-first-century Black Freedom Movement in terms of class, gender, and the politics of sexuality. These variables were central distinguishing features of the struggle, as reflected both in the narratives of those who were involved for a sustained period and in the vision and principles that the new groups eventually put forth. As progressive activist and St. Louis minister Rev. Osagyefo Sekou, who was a core organizer during the Ferguson protests, put it, "I take my orders from 23-year-old queer women."[30]

The stories of two other young activist women illustrate the ways in which Black feminist influence took hold in concrete ways. One is the political evolution of Johnetta (Netta) Elzie, a fierce young protestor (twenty-five years old at the time). Outraged over Brown's death, she hit the streets when the Ferguson uprising began, and never looked back. The events of August 2014 also changed her life. A native of Black working-class St. Louis, Elzie was politicized in large part through social media, and Twitter became the primary medium for her activism. Enraged by what had happened in her community, having already lost a personal friend to police violence, Elzie unleashed a steady stream of tweets after Brown's death, first to express her own anger and frustration and then to mobilize others to act. Early on in the protests, she met, befriended, and joined forces with Baltimore native DeRay Mckesson, who had quit his job as an administrator for the controversial Teach for America program, had migrated to Ferguson, and eventually became one of the most well-known faces on social media loosely associated with what came to be termed the Black Lives Matter Movement, although he has never been a member of BLMGN and is not a member of M4BL.

In the immediate wake of Brown's murder, Elzie became ubiquitous on social media and ever present on the streets of Ferguson and in the planning meetings and debates that took place in local churches, in living rooms, and on street corners during those early, intensive days of the uprising. Her involvement propelled her into the national spotlight, where she landed on the cover of the *New York Times Magazine,* appeared as a guest on MSNBC, sat in meetings with politicians, and was featured in a glamorous spread in *Essence* magazine.[31]

Though Elzie was admittedly not an organizer or an activist before Brown's murder, her newfound calling thrust her into unexpected conversations, exposing her to ideas she had never encountered in quite the same way, and powerfully impacted her evolving worldview. A January 2015 interview in the *Atlantic* magazine chronicles this evolution: "When I went out on August 9, it wasn't because I was concerned with feminism. It was because I was concerned about black people," she pointed out bluntly.[32] But then she experienced two things that seemingly added a new dimension to her resolve. First, she observed Black men taking credit for the work of Black women organizers and usurping the mantle of leadership, when the majority of those she had seen on the streets most consistently were women. At the Ferguson protests, she had witnessed hundreds of Black women defying the cops and curfews and withstanding teargas and rubber bullets, but in her words, "When it was time to have meetings and private phone calls and the back door stuff[,] I'd go to these places and it would be predominantly male, predominantly heterosexual black men.... There would always be some man who would answer the question for me while I'm trying to talk."[33] This sexist behavior did not sit well with the outspoken young woman, who was coming into her own as an activist, and she did not hesitate to make her feelings known.

Second, she made new friends in the struggle, many of whom were Black feminists, and they talked with her "in great detail about feminism," explaining the differences between various and competing feminist traditions. Elzie was influenced by her Black feminist comrades and her own gender experiences within the movement. Black feminist politics impacted her thinking, even if she does not place herself fully in that tradition. She concluded the interview this way: "I have met some of the most brilliant, smart, and beautiful black women ever. And they've changed my life. I've never felt so empowered before.... It's nice to have sisterhood in struggle."[34] Even though Elzie may not label herself a feminist, the sentiments she expressed reverberate in the writings, speeches, and manifestos of Black feminists from the 1970s to the present.

The second story that exemplifies the influence of Black feminist ideas among Ferguson activists is the lesser-known story of Alisha Sonnier, who was already a socially conscious local teen leader before the uprising. As was the case with Elzie, Michael Brown's death touched her deeply. Years earlier Sonnier had organized protests with other Black youth, who were routinely profiled, hassled, and harassed at their local shopping mall near

Ferguson. She was aware of racism and was outspoken in standing up for herself and her friends, but she did not consider herself an organizer per se. Rather, she engaged in what most historians and movements and observers refer to as everyday acts of resistance. But that was the extent of it.[35]

When Michael Brown was killed, Alisha was eighteen years old, a recent high school graduate on her way to her first year of college at St. Louis University (SLU) in the fall of 2014. But echoing Elzie's sentiments, Sonnier notes that the uprising in Ferguson opened her eyes, and "changed my life," forever.[36] On the second day of the protests, she and three friends, including her boyfriend, Jonothan, having heard about Brown's death through social media, went down to Florissant Avenue, the epicenter of the protests, to see what was happening. Having heard a rumor of a vigil, they brought candles and expected that this would be the extent of their participation. As they approached what they thought would be a peaceful expression of mourning, they came upon a phalanx of heavily armed police. Immediately, Alisha knew this was different than any situation she had been in before.

A few minutes later, everything got very personal and even more dangerous. Jonothan, holding a sign that read "Freedom Ain't Free," began walking toward the police line. He and others marching with him were given a stark thirty-second warning to stop, but the police did not wait for him to comply. He was hit with pepper spray five seconds later and fell to the ground. Alisha wrapped his arm around her shoulder, and they limped toward the nearby home of a family friend, still not knowing what Jonothan had been doused with. "What's wrong with the young brother?" a neighbor asked. Jonothan was in excruciating pain. He kept saying his skin was on fire. He was burning up. The man brought out his water hose in an effort to provide temporary relief, but a few minutes later the burning returned with greater intensity. Finally, they found some milk and poured it over Jonothan's face, and the pain seemed to lessen. It was a startling wake-up call about the willingness of the state to use violence on unarmed Black protesters.[37]

Rather than being frightened and deterred by her encounter with police violence on the streets of Ferguson, Alisha was emboldened, and her sense of purpose was fortified. She dug in. She attended strategy meetings at St. John's Church, one of the key meeting places; went out into the streets night after night; and found her voice. When college classes began that fall, she and her fellow students, along with community members, organized "Occupy SLU," a massive encampment that essentially shut down the private Catholic university campus for an entire week until a set of thirteen demands were agreed to by the university administration. Working with Tribe X, a group of young Black activists (which she cofounded in the thick of the struggle); the Metropolitan St. Louis Coalition for Inclusion and Equality; and the SLU Black Student Alliance, Alisha was at the center of the occupation, and it was a powerful learning experience. But that was only the beginning of her growing political commitment.[38]

As Alisha's understanding and political engagement deepened, and after she had a few hard-fought battles under her belt, she found issues of gender to be increasingly important to her in the context of this Black-led struggle against police violence. In reflecting back on her participation in the Ferguson protests a year and a half later, she was eager to recount not only the specific details of the street actions—the arrests and the late-night confrontations with the police—but also the ways in which her attitude and passion on a whole range of issues had expanded, especially regarding issues of gender and sexuality. "Sure, I had seen sexism before, but

I really got to see it in the movement ... the way the men treated us [at times, as black women] was like our lives didn't matter."[39]

Alisha experienced a kind of protective paternalism when some male leaders told women they should go home, implying they were not tough enough to be in the streets after dark. Her response was "I don't need you to try to push me to the back. I don't need you to erase me. I don't need you to silence me."[40] There were also subtle and not-so-subtle forms of harassment and disrespect in the rough-and-tumble demonstrations and in the sometimes chaotic and unscripted meeting and social spaces. In some instances, men were literally "grabbing booties," she recalled. "And we had to say, 'Hey, brothers, don't do that. We are not out here for that.'"[41] Alisha overheard some men refer to Black women who had rebuffed their sexual advances as "bitches."

In another instance, she overheard fellow male protesters mock and malign the relationship of a lesbian couple that had become prominent in the struggle: "They are just playing. They can't be getting satisfied," the men quipped. Alisha was highly upset and offended by these remarks, even though before her involvement in the movement, she had never been in political or social spaces with openly same-sex couples. She bristled at the hypocrisy of fellow protesters who would chant "black lives matter" one minute and disrespect straight women and queer women the next. She recognized other contradictions as well. How dare they, she thought to herself, not see the double standard in sagging their pants as a style statement and then criticizing young women who wore short skirts or "twerked" at parties as "hoes." She did not hesitate to speak out when she witnessed and overheard such things.[42]

Through readings, teach-in discussions, and personal conversations with others involved in the struggle, Alisha began to explore broader, deeper, and far-reaching questions about the nature of oppression, injustice, and power. In the wake of her participation, and as a direct outgrowth of the Ferguson uprising, she began to develop a Black feminist point of view. Out of all the people who flooded into Ferguson to support the protest movement there, Alisha had been most intrigued and influenced by groups of women who were talking about gender and sexuality. In her words, they were critiquing the heterosexual binary of "good girls" versus "bad girls" imposed on Black (and other) women. Why couldn't there be greater sexual expression and sexual freedom and autonomy, she began to wonder.[43]

On one level, murder by police and sexual freedom for Black women may seem like unrelated issues, but for young Black feminists, they were intimately related. For Alisha, fighting for liberation and freedom from police violence and harassment had raised the large and unwieldy questions, What freedom are we fighting for? And whose freedom are we fighting for? In other words, when protesters insist "Let's get free," do they mean free from just police abuse or something much more? For Alisha and most of those who have sustained their involvement, the answer is the latter.[44]

When the Department of Justice (DOJ), under heavy pressure from activists, conducted a six-month investigation of the Ferguson city government and police department, a portrait was painted that revealed even more of the backstory to Wilson's confrontation with Michael Brown on that fateful summer day. The story was indeed much bigger than those two men. The DOJ documented what Black Ferguson residents already knew. Steady and consistent harassment and intimidation of the town's residents, 67 percent of whom were Black, were perpetrated by an essentially all-white police force. In fact, harassing, arresting, and fining African American residents of the town had become a nefarious revenue source.

The DOJ declared, "Police Department and court operated not as independent bodies but as a single money making venture. Investigators found that officers stopped and arrested people without cause and used excessive force almost exclusively against African-Americans."[45] Fines from misdemeanor violations and traffic offenses were used to fill municipal coffers at the expense of Black citizens. The majority-Black population of Ferguson felt under siege from a callous group of white cops and city officials, who saw them all as a resource to be ruthlessly exploited, as well as being some version of Michael Brown—that is, less than human. The situation in Ferguson resembled the segregated, racist-run hamlets of the Jim Crow South.

The many people I talked to who were active on the streets of Ferguson during what we now look back on as the historic 2014 uprising all insisted that to understand Ferguson, we have to look at the larger St. Louis area. St. Louis is a Rust Belt city that has suffered economically over the past few decades. Loss of jobs and housing has hit the city hard. The area surrounding the community center where the Organization for Black Struggle has its headquarters is physically devastated: dilapidated homes, vacant lots, and empty storefronts. This neighborhood is an extension of Ferguson. This is the backdrop against which the police violence and community resistance played out. The thirty-five-year-old OBS had been on the scene fighting these conditions long before the Ferguson uprising occurred and continued to play a leadership role during and after the uprising. Respected local leaders like OBS's Montagne Simmons were on the streets day and night providing guidance, advice, and support to protesters. Jamala Rogers recalls that when the protests began, "Those already in the trenches ... shifted into the role that best utilized their skills and talents."[46]

Where there are large Black populations, high unemployment, crumbling infrastructure, and an active underground
economy, there is heavy-handed policing, which takes different
forms. So-called broken windows policing, a racist and highly
flawed model, has been the modus operandi of the Chicago and
New York police forces and many others across the country for
years.[47] The supposed logic maintains that smaller, seemingly
benign offenses portend serious crimes, and tackling the former
will prevent the latter. In other words, there is criminal behavior
and "precriminal" behavior. This mind-set sets the stage for
racial profiling and harassment of entire groups of people, who
"might" be headed toward serious crimes. Michael Brown's
treatment at the hands of Ferguson police is an example of
where this approach can lead: a petty, or perceived, infraction
leads to confrontation and deadly results.

The initial phase of the Ferguson uprising sustained itself for
about two weeks. Braving teargas, pepper spray, rubber bullets,
and the intimidating presence of the National Guard, local protesters were bolstered by outside allies, who filled the streets of
Ferguson, defying the curfew with ferocious, spirited demonstrations. Given the number of people in the streets—unaffiliated, unorganized, and with varying levels of political consciousness—it is perhaps surprising that more random acts of
vandalism and looting did not occur. But looting was indeed a
small-scale part of the rebellion, a part that mainstream media
and local officials latched onto in a feeble attempt to discredit
the protests overall. It did not work. While some mainstream
leaders took the bait and cleaved the protesters into good and
bad actors, most did not do so successfully or effectively.

Even the media were divided. Commentators like Van Jones on
CNN and Melissa Harris-Perry and Joy Reid on MSNBC ques-

tioned the ways in which more conservative Black journalists like CNN's Don Lemon seemed to equate violence against people with violence against property. The "politics of respectability," a layered and complex notion, is a longstanding mode of isolating and marginalizing those sectors of the Black community who do not conform to middle-class norms of behavior and comportment.[48] In the 1940s, civil rights organizer Ella Baker cautioned against excluding the so-called town drunk from campaigns for civil rights for fear that his or her presence would somehow discredit the movement—as if proper behavior and politeness have ever protected Black people from discrimination or racial violence. For some observers, the rowdiness of the Ferguson crowds seemingly eclipsed the righteousness of their grievances. Positing another view, political scientist Fredrick Harris describes the politics of respectability and its relevance in this way:

> What started as a philosophy promulgated by black elites to "uplift the race" by correcting the "bad" traits of the black poor has now evolved into one of the hallmarks of black politics in the age of Obama, a governing philosophy that centers on managing the behavior of black people left behind in a society touted as being full of opportunity. In an era marked by rising inequality and declining economic mobility for most Americans—but particularly for black Americans—the twenty-first-century version of the politics of respectability works to accommodate neoliberalism. The virtues of self-care and self-correction are framed as strategies to lift the black poor out of their condition by preparing them for the market economy.[49]

In other words, the principle of the politics of respectability is to advocate individual solutions to systemic problems and, conversely, to blame individual "bad" behavior and mistakes for system-wide conditions of racism and poverty.

A radical politics of intersectionality insists not only that marginalized sectors of oppressed communities be included in any political calculus for liberation but that their suffering, interests, and aspirations be at the very center of any movement concerned with social transformation. Those marginalized subjects include not only those deemed disreputable as sexual subjects, but others as well, which is why the new movements' emphasis on class is also significant. Looters, for example, are stigmatized in another way: dismissed as "thugs" or "riff raff," they are deemed undeserving of the rights supposedly afforded to law-abiding citizens. However, there is a political lens through which we can view a practice as controversial and seemingly random as looting. Poor people understand that an aspect of social control in a class society defined by gaping disparities in wealth is that police protect property, sometimes at the expense of the well-being of people. There is an armed line of demarcation between poor people and the things they cannot have but often need and deserve. When law and order break down, so does that line of demarcation. To make the point more bluntly, when homeless people occupy empty buildings, they are arrested for violating the property rights of absentee owners, and when hungry people invade a local grocery store and make off with food to feed their children, they too are punished by the state, even if the excess inventory was about to be discarded. The injustice of police violence against Black bodies is seen as contiguous with the everyday threat of violence that prevents the working poor, unemployed, and underemployed from having food, clothes, or even small luxury items that are dangled in front of them every day by the multi-billion-dollar advertising industry. Looting, in some people's minds, may at least temporarily jettison that unjust arrangement. It is ironic but perhaps not terribly surprising that looting is sometimes portrayed as an even greater evil than the loss of human life.

The Ferguson uprising made international headlines and had a ripple effect across the country. Those who reflexively showed up in Ferguson days after the protests began included filmmakers and journalists, veteran activists, religious leaders, and ordinary folk who wanted to stand with the people of Ferguson. Young organizers showed up—like thirty-four-year-old New Yorker Maurice (Moe) Mitchell. Moe and others began to strategize alongside locals about ways to lengthen the reach of the Ferguson uprising and connect it to other struggles. Mitchell arrived in August and stayed through December. His role in stitching together local and national efforts was vital.

He arrived in Ferguson and immediately reconnected with St. Louis activists he already knew and began to pitch in. Mitchell brought with him years of organizing experience in a number of progressive electoral and grassroots campaigns. He was among a small group of movement-builders who gravitated to the energy Ferguson generated, adding fuel to the fire that local people had lit. Mitchell walked up and down the streets of Ferguson and talked to people, facilitated meetings that brought various organizations together, conducted direct-action trainings, and tapped his national contact list to bring other organizations and resources to the aid of Ferguson protesters. In the thick of the fray, Mitchell tweeted from Ferguson on August 17, "No hyperbole. No exaggeration. This is a war zone. Why is our government so intent on silencing these young people?"[50] If the government was trying to silence them, Mitchell was determined to help amplify their voices.

Media from all over the world showed up to cover the Ferguson story. Palestinians halfway around the world watched the uprising on television, followed it through social media, and tweeted statements of solidarity. Banners shared on social media and held up by solidarity delegations that eventually visited Ferguson read, "Palestine Stands in Solidarity with Ferguson" and "Ferguson to Palestine, Occupation Is a Crime." Palestinians also sent practical messages about how protesters could protect themselves from the effects of teargas.[51] In South Africa (and London), there were solidarity actions that linked the injustices faced by Black people on that continent with the struggles of the people of Ferguson.

In the year after Brown's murder, demonstrations took place in over 150 cities. In New York City, the Justice League, a group cofounded by veteran civil rights activist Harry Belafonte, in conjunction with a dozen or so other groups, called for massive demonstrations. People spilled into the streets, filling Times Square and clogging the West Side Highway in Manhattan. They shut down the Brooklyn Bridge, tied up the George Washington Bridge, and disrupted Columbia University's campus. Some of the activity was organized, but not centrally, while some was purely spontaneous. There were no demonstration permits, no single leader galvanizing the masses, no premade signs that everyone carried. This was messy, and it was massive. Dozens of cities witnessed Black-led multiracial protests on a mass scale. Aerial views on news reports showed throngs of people marching through the streets of major cities, from Los Angeles to Chicago, in solidarity with Ferguson.

Clergy gave Black Lives Matter sermons and put banners on their churches. There were "White Coats for Black Lives" demonstrations by health providers and medical students. Then there was the formation of Law for Black Lives, which was organized by the Center for Constitutional Rights, and has now spun off as a freestanding group. And there were tiny community groups, student groups, groups of friends, and groups of activists in other struggles who made the Black Lives Matter slogan their own, scrawled it on handmade cardboard placards, and took it to the streets—engaging in civil disobedience on a large scale and disrupting business as usual. Some of these protests occurred in the immediate wake of Brown's murder, and some occurred after the grand jury verdict.

Anticipating correctly that the grand jury would decide not to indict Darren Wilson in the fall of 2014, the loose, local coalition of groups and individuals that had sustained the Ferguson protests called for a massive fall resistance campaign, which they called "Ferguson October." They invited caravans of supporters to join them. Even though the Darren Wilson decision would not be handed down until November, thousands still heeded the call to come to Ferguson in October. The hacker group Anonymous showed up and took credit for temporarily shutting down the Ferguson police department's website, threatening further actions. "You should have expected us," one of their signs read.[52] Legal teams came from the National Lawyers Guild, the Advancement Project, and the American Civil Liberties Union.

Organizers working against the inhumane deportation schemes of the US government immediately saw the Ferguson connection. Marisa Franco, leader of the national coalition Not One More, which has now evolved into Mijente, and a longtime friend of Alicia Garza's, stressed the political significance of having immigration organizers stand in solidarity with Ferguson. In an MSNBC article she authored entitled "Latino Communities Must See Ferguson's Fight as Their Own," Franco writes, "So much lip service is given to the idea of the 'black-brown' unity. This is an opportunity to go beyond theory and rhetoric. We learn infinitely more by doing, and we can build and fortify unity between our communities through joint struggle. A good ally shows up, and pushes what's moving and plugs in where help is needed. Let's listen carefully on how we can show up and contribute."[53] The same overpolicing policies used on Black communities have also been directed at communities of undocumented persons. Immigration and Customs Enforcement is the second-largest criminal investigative agency in the United States, and its detention prisons have rivaled the growth of state-run and private prisons, which have become a booming industry.[54]

The massive turnout for "Ferguson October" revealed a scale of sustained organizing and network building that made good on the often-repeated statement "This is a movement, not a moment." The signs people carried represented the breadth of the informal but far-reaching coalition that had grown up out of the soil of Ferguson. In addition to the signs linking Ferguson to Palestine and to immigrant rights were those of LGBTQIA groups, faith-based groups, prison abolitionists, and environmentalists. The progressive wing of the organized labor movement showed up as well. Service Employees International Union president Mary Kay Henry declared, "We stand with our brothers and sisters in Ferguson." She called for peaceful demonstrations at courthouses around the country to protest the nonindictment of Darren Wilson.[55]

Activists had already jettisoned the "All Lives Matter" challenge, which attempted to dilute and diffuse the potency of the Black Lives Matter message. Of course all lives matter, movement leaders responded, but this new movement was responding to the systematic devaluation of Black life in particular. If we were all equally vulnerable, there would be no need to underscore the importance of Black life, but that was clearly not the case. It was this understanding of the pervasiveness and persistence of anti-Black racism that was reflected in the eclectic mass of individuals and organizations that came together for the Ferguson demonstrations.

In the wake of #BlackLivesMatter's freedom rides to Ferguson, Garza, Tometi, and Khan-Cullors got together to explore what was next for their network and base. People who had participated in the rides asked them to set up some kind of organizational structure to continue and expand their efforts. This had not been their intent, but they conceded that something was needed. So the Black Lives Matter Network was born and morphed into the BLMGN. Chapters subscribe to a set of principles, but beyond that they are given a great deal of autonomy and freedom to define their priorities, their campaigns, and even their membership.[56] At the outset, some chapters, like Denver's, for example, even included non-Black members.

On the one hand, this loose structure represented a refreshing new approach to national leadership. On the other hand, it represented new and perhaps unexpected challenges. Alicia, Opal, and Patrisse were thrust into the spotlight as the term *Black Lives Matter* went viral. In a powerful essay entitled "A Herstory of the BlackLivesMatter Movement," Alicia insisted that the three founders not be erased from the origins of the term as it took off and began to be deployed in ways inconsistent with their intentions or politics.[57] After Ferguson, however, and even though the cofounders of #BLM and BLMGN insisted repeatedly that they were not personally leading or speaking for an entire movement, they often found themselves cast in that role; with that casting came lavish praise, harsh criticisms, and unrealistic expectations.

Predictably, the media erroneously conflated the BLMGN with the entire multifaceted movement. At the same time, others with no connection to the network's chapter structure or its leadership, and no connection to the myriad of organizations that legitimately fall under its larger banner, literally hijacked the mantle of BLM. This further complicated things. These were the so-called rogue BLM chapters, such as the Cuyahoga County "chapter" in Ohio that endorsed a Republican candidate for state senate to the horror and chagrin of the national BLMGN leadership, which immediately disavowed the group.[58]

A critical dilemma early on for BLMGN as it began to receive donations and grants to support its work was staffing. None of the three cofounders of BLMGN was ever on staff. However, they brought in longtime Oakland-area activist and leftist Ayoka Turner, then an advanced seminary student, to help with the work. She was hired and devoted considerable time and energy for the first two years, working to get the network established. Later, other staff were brought on board to handle communications and outreach and coordinate the chapter work. They were Nikita Mitchell, Miski Noor, Kandace Montgomery, Shanelle Matthews, and others. As of 2017, there is a solid chapter structure, decision-making procedures, and plans for internal leadership development. The network is still decentralized, but it rests on the work of a number of robust local chapters, including those in Chicago, Los Angeles, the Bay Area, and the Twin Cities.

In the wake of the Ferguson uprising, Black freedom organizing overall took on new urgency. Similar questions and dilemmas that faced BLMGN also faced the larger movement. So from the summer of 2014 to the spring of 2015, numerous meetings, formal and informal convenings, and retreats took up a range of questions. Some of these were closed strategy sessions involving different organizational representatives. However, the largest public movement gathering was in Ohio, one year after Michael Brown's death.

In Cleveland, in the summer of 2015, thousands gathered under the banner of the Movement for Black Lives, a new coalition in the making that had been formed the previous December to wrestle with critical questions facing the nascent movement of which BLMGN, BYP100, Million Hoodies, and Dream Defenders were a part. The tight-knit Blackbird collective, aided by activists on the ground in Cleveland, was instrumental in pulling together the historic conference at Cleveland State University, which took place July 24–26, 2015. The convening involved representatives from dozens of organizations in the planning process—a process that was politically and logistically challenging. While many groups were invited to help plan the conference, participation was, not surprisingly, uneven. The gathering drew a diverse crowd of over two thousand Black people from around the country, including Mississippi organizers from the Malcolm X Grassroots Movement, who hosted a dynamic workshop on their Cooperation Jackson campaign to transform and liberate that historic city. Other attendees included Black food justice organizer Dara Cooper; Black and Puerto Rican activist and Green Party former vice presidential candidate Rosa Clemente; filmmaker Byron Hurt; Oakland journalist Margaret Prescod; contingents from Million Hoodies United, Dream Defenders, Southerners on New Ground, Project South, and the James and Grace Lee Boggs Center in Detroit; and a contingent of Ferguson protesters. There was also a dynamic workshop by Paris Hatcher, the creative force behind Black Feminist Futures Project, a volunteer collective that hosts "visioning salons," to envision just futures, and media and cultural interventions that promote the leadership, empowerment, and amplified voices of Black women. Mariame Kaba of Project NIA and Page May with the We Charge Genocide collective facilitated a workshop about Chicago's "Reparations Now!" campaign, a successful crusade that culminated in a city ordinance providing reparations to victims of police torture. Some veteran Black feminist activists from the 1980s and '90s also showed up to lend support. There were at least two dozen members of the old Black Radical Congress present, as well as activists from INCITE! and Critical Resistance.

The emotional highlight of the Cleveland gathering was the opening session, which featured family members of and a photo tribute to dozens of victims of police violence. One by one, mothers, siblings, and children of those slain stepped forward and said the names of their loved ones, followed by "this is why I fight." Many in the audience were visibly shaken and rose to applaud at the end of the session, often with tears streaming down their faces. There was also a people's assembly, conducted with an audience of one thousand plus, led by Project South's Ash-Lee Henderson, the new codirector of the legendary Highlander Center in Tennessee as of 2017. She walked the crowd through a list of statements, asking for affirmation to measure the level of consensus on some core principles that would guide M4BL going forward. At the end of the two-day gathering, some people left with a mood of hopeful anticipation about what would come next, while some, disappointed that there were not more concrete outcomes, still wondered what level of unity was possible.[59] Echoing through the cavernous auditorium and energizing the crowd was the recorded sound of singer Kendrick Lamar's popular tune "Alright."

A smaller retreat was held a week later in upstate New York at the YWCA Conference Center, hosted by Alicia Garza and Linda Burnham of the National Domestic Workers Alliance under the banner "Now That We Got Love, What Are We Gonna Do?" The goal of that intergenerational gathering, which included civil rights movement icon Bob Moses, labor leader Gerry Hudson, movement elders Makani Themba and Jamala Rogers, and myself, as well as a hundred others, was to share analyses, try to make sense of the moment, and determine if a stronger consensus could be achieved among the diverse forces that had been assembled. It is important to note that Jamala and Makani played very special roles in the movement upsurge from the outset. Jamala was a central figure giving strategic advice and practical support in Ferguson, as a longtime St. Louis organizer. Makani was a national resource. Of her contribution, activist Ash-Lee Henderson says, "Makani Themba's commitment to sharing the lessons of past liberation movements, her clarity of this current political movement and our positionality in it, and her revolutionary vision for the future of our people has made her a crucial support and wise sister-elder. Our strategies and relationships are stronger because of her commitment to our leadership, relationships, and our building of successful and impactful movements."[60] Stories were shared and relationships were deepened, but much more work remained.

A year later, the effects of the Ferguson uprising against racist state violence were still being felt throughout the state and the country, when the flagship campus of University of Missouri, ninety miles from Ferguson, erupted in protest over racist incidents on campus. The school, located in Columbia, Missouri, but commonly referred to as Mizzou, was the site of a prolonged hunger strike, a boycott of classes, a tent city encampment, and large boisterous demonstrations. Many of the student leaders at Mizzou had visited the Ferguson protests, and others had been inspired from a distance. An activist group formed on campus calling itself "Concerned Students 1950," a reference to the year

Black students were finally admitted to Mizzou. Ultimately, when the predominately Black football team refused to play (foreshadowing the heroic actions of professional football player Colin Kaepernick who "took a knee," refusing to stand during the national anthem at games to protest racism and police violence) as a show of support for the protests, the university acceded to some of the students' demands, and the president and chancellor were both forced to resign. The year before the major Mizzou protests, a group of young Black women activists had laid some of the political foundations that made the large mobilization possible. The 2015 Mizzou protests were the most visible campus actions, but there were smaller rallies, vigils, and direct actions in solidarity with and as a part of BLMM/M4BL took place on nearly eighty campuses throughout the country.[61] An outgrowth of these disparate campus struggles was the formation of the Black Liberation Collective, a national network of Black student activists.[62]. In 2014–15 Missouri was a hub of resistance to anti-Black racism, influencing and inspiring political actions throughout the country. By the spring of 2015, Baltimore would become another center of protest.

FOUR

Black Rage and Blacks in Power

Baltimore and Electoral Politics

If the spurious argument that we live in a postracial society, and that Barack Obama's election represented the nail in the coffin of American racism, had any real traction among serious-minded people, the Black Lives Matter Movement and Movement for Black Lives (BLMM/M4BL) stopped that lie in its tracks and further underscored the lesson that neither representative politics nor charismatic leaders constitute a magic formula for liberation.

As I was growing up in Detroit in the early 1970s, in the wake of the 1967 rebellion—another uprising sparked by police violence—there was a horrific police decoy unit operating in the city at the time called S.T.R.E.S.S. The acronym stood for Stop the Robberies, Enjoy Safe Streets. White undercover cops would creep around Black neighborhoods, sometimes feigning intoxication, all but asking to be robbed in order to entrap young, would-be robbers. These setups also resulted in a number of back-alley shootings and violent arrests of Black Detroiters.[1] At the time, some of us naively felt that a desegregated police force populated by Black officers from our community would curb or eliminate police violence, and the election of the city's first Black mayor, Coleman Young, in 1974, would deal a decisive blow to racism and police violence in our city. We were wrong. The anti–police violence protesters in Ferguson, Oakland, Chicago, New York, and Baltimore in 2014 and 2015 knew better. Even if not everyone articulated the problem in these terms, their actions represented an understanding of the systemic nature of racism and the complex workings of a multiracial, white-supremacist, neoliberal state. In other words, this generation of Black activists has witnessed desegregated police forces, many more Black elected officials (including a Black man in the White House), and the growth of a Black millionaire class, but Black poverty, suffering, and vilification still exist, and they are increasingly class specific.

This understanding was most clear on the streets of Baltimore after the death in police custody of twenty-five-year-old Freddie Gray on April 19, 2015, eight months after the death of Michael Brown. Gray was arrested on a minor infraction, handcuffed, and literally tossed into the back of a police van, after which the officers reportedly took a deliberately bumpy route, presumably to teach Gray a lesson for whatever he had said or done. He died five days later, and the city erupted in protest. People poured into the streets by the thousands. Curfews were imposed and ignored, the Maryland National Guard was in the streets, and violent clashes took place between crowds and police. Cars were attacked, rocks were thrown, businesses were looted, and dozens of people were arrested. Baltimore in spring 2015 was the second major rebellion to follow a police killing in less than a year. But Baltimore was not Ferguson. In Baltimore the city's mayor, Stephanie Rawlings Blake, was Black, as were many of the city's police and elected officials, including the outspoken young Black female state's attorney, Marilyn J. Mosby.[2]

Gray's case was not a simple racial formula of white cop killing Black youth, as three of the six police officers indicted for
Gray's murder were black, including a Black woman. Given
these demographics, one might have expected activists to hesitate before making the allegation of racism. But they did not. It
was immediately clear to them that the problem was structural
racism, which included profiling and harassment of a certain
type of poor or working-class Black youth, an aggressive policing style in poor Black communities. That notorious blue code
of silence among cops, which often trumps any kind of racial
solidarity that Black officers might otherwise feel toward the
Black community, is very real.

Black political rage was on full display in Baltimore during
those days in April. Having witnessed the disastrous handling of
the Ferguson protests, Baltimore officials took a different
approach. Apologies were given, "preemptive" measures were
taken, concern was expressed for the Gray family, and community meetings were held. Still, protesters wore T-shirts that read
"Fuck the Police." And by all indications, they meant it.

After a series of high-profile police killings across the country—
Tamir Rice, Walter Johnson, John Crawford, Eric Garner, and
more—the Baltimore crowds were not in the mood for dialogue or
apologies. They were outraged and fed up. At the height of that
rage, Black elected officials and the nation's first Black president
counseled calm. In President Obama's words, "Anger is not always
productive. All too often it distracts attention from solving real
problems." In this case it was Black anger that had uncovered, and
forced national attention on, issues that had for too long been swept
under the rug.[3]

Rutgers University professor and outspoken Black feminist
scholar-activist Brittney Cooper captured this sentiment in her

provocative essay in *Salon* entitled "In Defense of Black Rage: Michael Brown, Police and the American Dream." She wrote, "No, I don't support looting. But I question a society that always sees the product of the provocation and never the provocation itself. I question a society that values property over black life. But I know that our particular system of law was conceived on the founding premise that black lives are white property."[4] Long before Ferguson and long before Baltimore, Dr. Martin Luther King Jr., the Black prophet of nonviolence, understood the underpinnings of Black rage when he said, "I could never again raise my voice against the violence of the oppressed in the ghettos without having first spoken clearly to the greatest purveyor of violence in the world today: my own government."[5]

In July 2016, as the movement was being castigated and disparaged for the actions of a lone Black gunman with a history of mental problems, who ambushed and killed five police officers in Dallas, BYP100 took the bold stance of defending Black rage and rejecting the criticisms being levied against the larger BLMM/ M4BL. On July 8, BYP100 issued a statement that indicted state violence and insisted that movement organizations should not back down or retreat from protests or organized campaigns in light of harsh and threatening criticisms: "Black rage is justified rage. Let us stay steadfast in our mission and stand unapologetically with our people."[6] They were in no way endorsing the sniper's actions, but at the same time they were not going to be intimidated into silence by those who sought to blame and indict BLMM/M4BL for actions they had nothing to do with.

Cooper, King, and BYP100 sought to put rage and rebellion in political and historical context while simultaneously confronting the hypocrisy of state actors, who deplore violence against property during mass protests but daily engage in practices that do violent harm on a large scale to human beings in the United States and around the world.

In Baltimore, as in Ferguson, spontaneous rebellion in the streets sparked the formation of new organizations and further energized existing ones. Two local organizations at the center of the protests after Freddie Gray's death Leaders of a Beautiful Struggle (LBS) and Baltimore Bloc. LBS was formed five years before Gray's death by newly politicized members of high school and college debate teams, who decided to apply their research and oratorical skills to community organizing. One of the founders, and its director of public policy, Dayvon Love, articulated a grassroots radical vision of Black politics, arguing that "those most affected must be in the leadership" of movement work, and "those of and from communities most affected must speak for ourselves."[7] LBS joined forces with Baltimore Bloc, the Baltimore Algebra Project, and others to form a new coalition. "Baltimore United for Change" represented a constellation of forces that occupied the Baltimore City Hall on Wednesday, October 14, 2015, to protest the confirmation of the unpopular Kevin Davis as the permanent Baltimore police commissioner. One of the principal organizers was Makayla Gilliam-Price, a dynamic teenage leader of a group called City Bloc. Gilliam-Price is the child of an activist family, whose parents were leaders of an anti–death penalty campaign to save her uncle's life in the late 1990s. Tyrone X. Gilliam, whom many believed was innocent of any crime, was executed on Maryland's notorious death row while Makayla was just a baby. Nearly two decades later, the family's fighting spirit continued in Makayla.[8]

During the city hall takeover, sixteen people were arrested after enduring harsh treatment at the hands of the Baltimore officials: bathrooms were closed, no food or water was allowed in, and finally the power was turned off. The sixteen were released Friday, October 16. LBS had also participated in an earlier campaign to prevent the building of a new hundred-million-dollar juvenile detention center, viewing it as yet another investment in what activists have critiqued as the school-to-prison pipeline.[9] LBS, it should be noted, has a different leadership model than many of the other groups discussed in this book. They opted for an LLC organizational model, rather than a nonprofit arrangement. They have a CEO, a COO, and various directors. In Love's view, this model gives his group more independence.[10]

The class divides within the Black community in Baltimore were on full display during the protests and factored in on a number of levels. First, there is the life story of Freddie Gray, who grew up poor and suffered from lead poisoning as a child, which impacted him the rest of his life.[11] Local organizers like Love, a child of working-class Baltimore residents, understood the interrelated nature of race and class in the lives of the city's Black poor. He also understood that whether the local officials were Black or white was not the decisive factor in making a change. In a television interview, Love observed, "People reduce racism to individual white folks in leadership. Baltimore shows the sophistication of white supremacy. How it takes black figures, puts them in institutional positions to give the veneer of justice when really the same institutional arrangement exists."[12]

Baltimore Bloc, an antiracist, multiracial formation, was another group that responded to Freddie Gray's death. Some of its members were arrested along with members of LBS, and others, in the protests that followed. They were also involved in protesting police killings before Gray's high-profile death. In July 2013, young Tyrone West was killed by Baltimore cops attempting to take him into custody.[13] Baltimore Bloc became close to the family and helped to keep West's case in the public eye. Protests around this case were ongoing as the tragedy of Freddie Gray's death played out. Baltimore Bloc had also organized around homelessness and policing. However, in 2014 after the Ferguson uprising, Black activists Ralikh Hayes, Tre Murphy, and Michaela Brown joined the group to lend their organizing skills, building upon the work of founders Duane "Shorty" Davis and Payam Sohrabi. Brown and others have since left Baltimore Bloc to found Baltimore Leaders Organizing for Change.[14]

While explicit and highly visible feminist leadership may not have been involved in the Baltimore struggle, as it was in other contexts, gender still played a role. The fact that two of the most powerful politicians in the city, and one of the cops implicated in Gray's death, were Black women militates against any simple formula that would put all Black people on the same side. Women were also prominent in the streets. And when the Department of Justice report on Baltimore came out after months of investigation, it revealed, not surprisingly, that women were also being harassed, profiled, and abused by the Baltimore police. The report indicated that Baltimore officers sometimes treated with contempt women who tried to report sexual assault. One victim was referred to by an officer as "a conniving little whore."[15] Even though in Baltimore, as elsewhere, the cases of police "misconduct" that grabbed public attention were those involving male victims, numerous, lesser-known, female victims suffered similarly. Their cases, however, were rarely elevated to the level of national protest. This was the message of the #SAYHERNAME campaign, which will be taken up in the next chapter.

Sixteen months after Freddie Gray's death, twenty-three-year-old Korryn Gaines, a Black mother of two, was shot dead by Baltimore County police, revealing another aspect of the racial and gendered nature of state violence. The shooting occurred inside Gaines's apartment just outside Baltimore in Randallstown, Maryland. She was killed on August 1, 2016, in the presence of her five-year-old son, who was also injured by police in the fray. The police were trying to serve a bench warrant for a simple traffic violation and another misdemeanor. Gaines, like many Americans, was a gun owner. She also had a strong sense of individual liberty and had had previous run-ins with the police, during which she felt her rights were being violated.[16] She believed in the right to bear arms and in the right to self-defense, as she expressed in cell phone videos and Facebook posts, which provide glimpses into Gaines's political views.[17] She was outraged by police killings of unarmed Black people, thought she was a potential victim, and was determined not to be "kidnapped" or killed without a fight.

Clearly, some of Gaines's views may have been unorthodox. For example, in lieu of her state-issued license plate, which she argued authorities had wrongly confiscated, her car carried a cardboard sign that read simply, "Free Traveler."[18] This makeshift plate had precipitated her earlier encounter with the police. Whatever one thinks about Gaines's ideas or her tactics of resistance to an authority she felt was unjust, she surely did not, activists insisted, deserve to be executed in front of her child because of those beliefs.

When police arrived at Gaines's home that ominous August day, she refused to let them in and indicated she was armed. After a seven-hour standoff, police opened fire on Gaines, who returned fire and was killed within minutes. No officers were hurt. Two months later, seven antigovernment followers of white ranchers Cliven and Ammon Bundy were acquitted after a six-week armed standoff, in which they seized control of government lands in a federal wildlife reserve in Oregon. They were not given the death penalty for their armed confrontation with government forces; rather, their actions were judged legally justified, and they were eventually set free.[19] As one headline read, "Sovereign law made Cliven Bundy a 'patriot' but Korryn Gaines 'crazy.'"[20] The contrast and similarities between the two cases are striking. What is also striking is the venomous comments and mocking condemnation of Gaines on social media by whites and a handful of Blacks, who suggested her alleged stupidity and recklessness resulted in her death. Whether Gaines had a diagnosable mental illness, which some have speculated on but her family denies, psychological stress owing to her life circumstances (she had been a victim of domestic violence), or an unshakeable conviction that she was living in an oppressive society with few resources to fight back, she did not deserve to be murdered.

Protests for Korryn Gaines were smaller than for Freddie Gray, but Black feminists were in the lead. They argued that as a Black woman she had been condemned and vilified for her resolve not to be broken. Whatever she had done, Gaines had not injured or killed anyone and did not fire the first shot in her fatal encounter with the police in her own home. A large sector of the movement, wedded to a rejection of respectability politics, refused to write Korryn Gaines off or devalue the loss of her life because she was not a perfect victim. A few days after the incident, BYP100's Charlene Carruthers wrote an impassioned essay in *Colorlines* magazine entitled "In Defense of Korryn Gaines, Black Women and Children."[21] She used Gaines's case as a launching point to talk about the vulnerability of Black women and children in a society that pathologizes Black mothers and their families. When BYP100 members joined a civil disobedience action in front of the Fraternal Order of Police offices in Baltimore some months later, in solidarity with Baltimore Bloc organizers, they wore T-shirts that read, "Remember Korryn."

Another group that emerged in the wake of Ferguson and defended Korryn Gaines's memory was Black Feminist Futures, a small network initiated by Atlanta-based artist-activist Paris Hatcher. When Gaines was killed, Black Feminist Futures organized and encouraged others to organize altars in her memory. Dozens of them sprung up in public and private spaces around the country and were sites for numerous vigils.

Black Feminist Futures has also hosted "visioning salons," borrowed from Black surrealists of the early twentieth century and very much a part of the larger Afrofuturist movement, to imagine alternative futures and create space for Black joy and healing amid a movement born of pain and trauma. This work is situated within a BLMM/M4BL culture that has embraced self-care, healing, and spiritual practices as tools for sustaining movement work.[22]

While the Baltimore uprising began as an expression of Black rage in the wake of Gray's death, Black officials had a dual approach—harshly condemning the militant protesters and feigning empathy for the peaceful ones. Marilyn Mosby, the young Black prosecutor, who indeed enjoyed community support and was considered progressive, held a press conference announcing she would prosecute the six implicated officers. "I heard your calls for 'no justice, no peace!'" she said in direct response to the protesters.[23] The implied promise was of justice, but the outcome fell short in the eyes of many. All of the officers implicated in Gray's death were charged, but eventually all either were acquitted or had the charges against them dropped.[24] The damning Department of Justice report on Baltimore's policing practices was issued on August 10, 2016. It concluded, in part, "BPD [Baltimore Police Department] engages in a pattern or practice of ... making unconstitutional stops, searches, and arrests [and] using enforcement strategies that produce severe and unjustified disparities in the rates of stops, searches and arrests of African Americans; using excessive force; and retaliating against people engaging in constitutionally-protected expression."[25] The struggle in Baltimore continues.

The Baltimore uprising, if nothing else, highlighted the limits of simply getting Black politicians elected to office or having Black people generally in positions of formal power. It occurred just as the US presidential primaries unfolded—a historic election that witnessed the ascendance of an openly socialist candidate, a serious female contender on the Democratic side, and an unscrupulous and unorthodox right-winger on the Republican side. The new wave of Black activists and organizers who came up in Ferguson, Baltimore, and beyond sought to engage this new electoral landscape on their own terms. But that electoral reckoning was not straightforward.

The issues raised by BLMM/M4BL had been forced to the forefront of public discourse and had to be addressed by politicians in the 2016 race, even if, in the case of Republicans, it was to castigate and vilify the movement. On the Democratic side, both primary frontrunners, Hillary Clinton and Bernie Sanders, appealed to the mass base of BLMM/M4BL and expressed sympathy for its goals, although not always its tactics. Most movement organizations and leaders weighed in on the issues of the election—challenging, critiquing, and publicly educating the candidates but refraining from any formal endorsements (with a few exceptions).[26] They also paid careful attention to local races without making major investments in the presidential campaigns. When asked, all of them were clear in their opposition to Trump, although they varied in their assessments of the likelihood that he would win. They refused at the same time to be uncritical cheerleaders for either Clinton or Sanders, both of whom, they argued, failed to offer a robust and convincing agenda for combatting racism. Bernie, although he clearly had a radical economic agenda, seemed philosophically just not to get it when it came to race. And most young Black activists did not trust Hillary because of her longstanding history with Wall Street and the Democratic Party machine, combined with her 1990s superpredator statement.

There were two critical moments during the 2015–16 presidential primary when BLMM/M4BL activists disrupted events at which Bernie Sanders was speaking to put issues of anti-Black violence and structural racism on the table: a Netroots Nation event in Arizona and a Sanders rally in Seattle a few weeks later. At the Netroots event in Phoenix on July 18, 2015, Black Alliance for Just Immigration organizer Tia Oso seized the microphone and the stage to confront Sanders and former Maryland governor Martin O'Malley about their weak stances on police brutality and racism. BLMGN cofounder Patrisse Khan-Cullors and others took part in the action as well. As Joe Dinkin wrote in *The Nation,* "[Bernie] had the opportunity to rewrite his own narrative and expand his base and he failed."[27] On August 8, 2015, despite being booed and heckled by liberal whites in the Seattle audience, two bold and articulate Black women commandeered the microphones to point out issues that candidates were not addressing with rigor. This should have been an opportunity for Sanders to embrace a more forceful antiracist platform, but he didn't.[28] At the same time, if Sanders had managed to earn a more solid Black vote in the primary, and if he had been the Democratic candidate for president in 2016, the Left and BLMM/M4BL would have been fighting a different, more winnable battle postelection. Everything else said, and all criticisms wholly justified, Sanders was one of the most radical presidential contenders for a major party nomination that the US electorate has seen since the Jesse Jackson bids in 1984 and 1988. Sadly, in the wake of the primaries, Sanders was sucked into the vortex of the corporatist Democratic Party and endorsed the opponent he had so eloquently critiqued, all of which was a setback for the prosocialist momentum of his campaign.

Several months before the November 2016 election, and just as the Movement for Black Lives was releasing its massive policy statement as a challenge to elected officials and candidates alike, Alicia Garza offered the following overview of her, and by extension much of the movement's, assessment of electoral politics and the two-party system as they relate to social movements: "What we've seen is an attempt by mainstream politics and politicians to co-opt movements that galvanize people in order for them to move closer to their own goals and objectives.... We don't think that playing a corrupt game is going to bring change and make Black lives matter."[29]

There has been much reassessing and soul-searching within BLMM/M4BL circles since the election of Donald Trump in November 2016. While most movement organizers still seem skeptical of mainstream politics, creative approaches to electoral strategy have emerged, as reflected in the M4BL's newly formed Electoral Justice Project (EJP), headed by Jessica Byrd, Rukia Lumumba, and Kayla Reed, and Alicia Garza's new Black Futures Lab, which has an electoral component that will conduct a massive survey of Black political opinion, dubbed "The Black Census."[30] Jessica Byrd's experience with the consulting, coaching, and training firm Three Point Strategies, which helps communities build successful electoral campaigns, has been an anchor for M4BL's entry into electoral work. Byrd began working on political campaigns as a teenager. She is a Black queer feminist, and she brings who she is to her work. A savvy optimist, she still has no illusions that elections alone will liberate Black people. She is convinced that by identifying the right candidates, mobilizing voters, and connecting with movement strategists, electoral work can make a difference.

Finally, the historic election of Chokwe Antar Lumumba, a thirty-six-year-old Black lawyer with family roots in the Black liberation struggle, as mayor of Jackson, Mississippi—on the promise of making Jackson "the most radical city on the planet"—means new possibilities are in the air.[31] Most agree that none of this work in the electoral arena should supplant grassroots organizing and movement-building, if Black working-class people are going to see anything that approximates freedom and justice. In addition, organizers have already experienced the dead-end political results when social movements working in marginalized communities forfeit their agency and simply deliver votes to politicians without a strategy or a plan for ensuring accountability. Acute awareness of the limits of the current electoral system is shared by organizations across the BLMM/M4BL network. Still, most savvy organizers are using an array of tools and tactics in pursuit of their goals.

"Rage" is often deemed irrational and unproductive, in need of containment and suppression. But there is such a thing as righteous rage: fury and indignation that fuels constructive, rather than destructive, action. In Chicago's #ByeAnita campaign, for example, it was the mobilization of Black anger that realized a just electoral outcome, the ouster of a state's attorney deemed by many to be racist and unresponsive to community concerns. It is Black rage, combined with strategic demands, that has pushed politicians to make at least minimal concessions to the call for greater police accountability in cities where protests have occurred. Rage is not always ineffective. If channeled and mobilized, collective rage can be simply the refusal to tolerate the intolerable. And that refusal can show up in many forms, from the streets to the polls.

FIVE

Themes, Dilemmas, and Challenges

Many themes, dilemmas, and challenges have created both tensions and opportunities for growth within the Black Lives Matter Movement and Movement for Black Lives (BLMM/M4BL) nationally. This chapter will briefly highlight six of them: 1) the reassertion of a politicized Black identity, 2) the power and limits of social media and new communications strategies, 3) intergenerational organizing and youth leadership, 4) Black feminist influences, 5) abolitionist practices of accountability, and 6) the class politics of the movement, including tensions over money. Since a movement by definition is an eclectic mix of distinct forces moving in a coordinated direction, there is no "party line" or rigid ideology, but there are shared assumptions, values, and analyses, in addition to struggles over which of the narratives, theories, and demands will move to center stage. This chapter will touch on some of the internal differences, as well as the common ground on which movement organizers stand.

"UNAPOLOGETICALLY BLACK"

The term *unapologetically Black,* coined initially by Fresco Steez (Angie Rollins), popularized by BYP100, and taken up by others, has become one of the mantras for this movement. It appears in chants, in speeches, on T-shirts, and on social media. It has also popped up in some very unlikely places. For example, *Fortune* magazine reprinted a speech by Mellody Hobson, the Black president of Ariel Investments and the wife of multibillionaire film mogul George Lucas, in which she also embraced the term. After attending the funeral of John Johnson, founder of *Ebony* and *Jet* magazines, Hobson recounted having an epiphany. In her words, one of the eulogists got up and said, "He [Johnson] was unapologetically black." "It hit me so hard," she recalled. She then admitted to herself, "[I had] been apologizing for who I am, about being a woman, and about being black—and it stops today."[1] Hobson's rather striking reality check is revealing on many levels. What it seems to suggest is that one of the common prerequisites for individual Black success has been that Black elites like Hobson, though they may engage in facile gestures of kinship, often effectively distance themselves from the suffering and struggles of the mass of ordinary Black people. In fact, success sometimes depends on their proving themselves "different" and apart from the mass of ordinary Black people. That distancing can be both physical and psychological. For wealthy and privileged Blacks in the late twentieth and twenty-first centuries, downplaying or apologizing for one's "blackness" does not necessarily mean "passing" for white, as light-skinned Blacks might have done generations ago. Rather, it means expressing political and class loyalty, as a condition of acceptance by wealthy white counterparts. That choice can be masked by charitable gestures, by support for modest liberal reforms, or by an aesthetic nod to African or African American cultural or artistic projects, but the choice remains the same. What being unapologetically Black now means for Mellody Hobson in her newly awakened state we do not know, but we know it means something quite different for thousands of newly minted young Black organizers, who have lifted up the term and deploy it in their organizing work.

Thousands of digital media agitators, local organizers, and street protesters have made the term *unapologetically Black* nearly as ubiquitous as *Black Lives Matter*. They are, at the most basic level, rejecting the fiction of a postracial world. Instead, they are foregrounding all the ways in which anti-Black attitudes and practices still exist and are refracted through the prisms of gender, sexuality, citizenship status, and class.And perhaps most significantly, they are refusing to disassociate from the common experience of ordinary Black folk, rejecting the idea that they should somehow be embarrassed (as the now-disgraced Bill Cosby once suggested they should be) by the Black poor.[2]

Unapologetically Black also tests the limits of the generic, amorphous, and sometimes confounding political category "people of color," which covers a vast range of diverse experiences, cultures, national identities, phenotypes, and, most important, relations to power and oppression. Unapologetically Black acknowledges that blackness is rooted in a particular political and historical context with bloody roots in the transatlantic slave trade, colonialism, slavery, and Jim Crow (old and new). It exists as the ultimate antithesis of white supremacy, the ideological anchor of racial capitalism. But it also acknowledges something else—that is, the positive aspects of a shared connection to an African American past. These include the strength that comes from resilience, resistance, and collective survival practices. While the dominant culture still denigrates and exoticizes dark skin, and pathologizes many Black social and cultural practices, BLMM/M4BL gatherings often start or end with the song "I Love Being Black" written by BYP100 member JeNae Taylor, a twenty-first-century version of "Say It Loud— I'm Black and I'm Proud," which resonated for the 1960s and '70s generations.

Increasingly as the erroneous notion of "postracialism" crept into popular discourse and the vernacular in the early 2000s, those concerns specific to poor and working-class Black communities were either buried in language about an eclectic set of communities of color or mentioned defensively. Organizers who focused on the particularities of Black oppression were often accused of reinforcing a Black-white binary. While the term *people of color* emerged in a political context as a laudable call to unity, a recognition of the global uses of white supremacy in pursuit of empire, and an understanding of the violence and suffering enacted upon the people of the Global South, it also sometimes obscures the myriad differences that reside within that large and unwieldy category. Teasing out and better understanding these differences are important components of building principled multiracial, multiethnic coalitions.

Unapologetically Black as a slogan is also a counterpoint to Barack Obama's ambivalent relationship to blackness. During one of the 2008 Democratic primary debates, that ambivalence was revealed with painful clarity. It was when then-Senator Obama was forced to choose between being accepted by an overwhelmingly white electorate and Democratic Party power brokers, or affirming his relationship to his longtime spiritual leader, radical Black pastor the Reverend Jeremiah Wright of Chicago's Trinity Church.

Obama initially hedged but eventually came out and vehemently "denounced" Wright, the man who had married the Obamas, baptized their children, and counseled the future president many times. The title of Barack Obama's bestselling book, *The Audacity of Hope,* was borrowed from the title of one of Wright's sermons.[3] Beginning in the 1970s, the mantra of Wright's church and the sign that stood in front of it proclaimed, "Unashamedly Black and Unapologetically Christian."[4] It is important to note that not only is Wright known for his progressive and radical views on race and racism (from initiating one of the first AIDS ministries to opening his church to antiapartheid organizations when few others would), but he is also a longstanding advocate of peace, is prolabor, and is committed to economic justice issues.[5] So Obama's choice to disassociate from Wright was as much political as it was racial. It represented a decisive break with the left-leaning politics that had influenced Obama as a young community organizer, as well as with the Black radical tradition. His speeches mocking and chastising "Cousin Pookie" for laziness and telling Black college students that racism should not be an "excuse" for failure are evidence of Obama's adherence to a twenty-first-century politics of respectability. While Obama continued to enjoy soul music, admire Black artists and athletes, and express himself occasionally in Black urban vernacular, his political break with the Black working class—except as loyal voters—was clear.

SOCIAL MEDIA AND NEW TECHNOLOGIES

The second critical theme for understanding this phase of the Black Freedom Movement is the new digital technology. Social media is the place where news of outrageous injustices is disseminated and people are called to action. It is the soapbox and public square of this generation, where many of the debates about strategy, tactics, and ideas are argued out in sound-bite form, for good or ill. In many ways, it is where BLMM/M4BL was incubated.

Most people first learned of Michael Brown's death through Twitter or Facebook. The fatal police shooting of twelve-year-old Tamir Rice in a park near downtown Cleveland, videotaped on a police dash camera, went viral on the Internet and triggered protests. Eric Garner's violent strangulation death by police after he tried to break up a fight between two other men in Staten Island, New York, was sent out to social media months after his death, which is when the case got significant attention and support. Unarguably, social media has had a powerful and profound impact as a communication tool that lends itself to democratic and inclusive practices of discourse, as well as to distortion and manipulation. It can serve to mobilize, publicize, bypass a disinterested mainstream media, and force issues into the public eye, or it can serve antithetical and nefarious purposes.

Some observers have labeled social media activists "citizen journalists," who report and disseminate stories that the mainstream press might otherwise ignore or distort.[6] Without their incessant tweets to update a global public on the Ferguson uprising, the support and solidarity actions that took place in hundreds of cities might not have occurred. Without an unwavering observer with a cell phone and a Facebook account, the police execution of Walter Scott, shot in the back while running away after a traffic stop in South Carolina, might have been erroneously reported as an act of self-defense, which was the official account of the officer who shot him. Most dramatic of all were the live Facebook feeds that captured the July 6, 2016, deadly police shooting of Philando Castile in a St. Paul, Minnesota, suburb as he sat in the car with his girlfriend, Diamond Reynolds, and her young daughter. The vivid and visceral images fueled anger and propelled people to action. They also jolted many white Americans, putting a reality in front of them that many had not seen before and might not have believed had it not been on their computer and cell phone screens.

Twitter in particular has become a special kind of public square for African Americans, who use the medium in a higher concentration than their white counterparts—so much so that the Black online communities that follow, engage, and retweet one another are sometimes referred to as "Black Twitter." Much of this back and forth, involving hundreds of thousands of users, is about nonpolitical topics. However, the community can be mobilized when political events occur.[7]

The immediate and unfiltered character of social media messaging is part of its power and danger. While Twitter and Facebook have been tools for movement building, they have also been sites for some nasty exchanges, for accusations, for name-calling, and for shaming. Within the large, eclectic, and occasionally fractious world of Black Twitter, there have even been threats. Some of these fights have revolved around politics and tactics, and some seem to have been painfully personal.

DeRay Mckesson is one of the most prominent social media personalities to emerge out of the Ferguson moment. With hundreds of thousands of followers on Twitter, a high-profile presence at major protests, and numerous media appearances, for which he nearly always wears his signature blue Patagonia vest, Mckesson has become his own brand. Appearing regularly on national media as a kind of self-appointed spokesperson, he seems to some observers to be shamelessly self-promoting. As Patrisse Khan-Cullors put it, he has "celebritized the movement." Mckesson, a Baltimore native, was at the center of some of the most pivotal events of the BLMM/M4BL protests. He made sacrifices, suffered harassment and arrests, and became a strong voice against police violence.[8] What he did not do was join forces with the hundreds of organizers who formed the M4BL coalition. While hundreds of M4BL members sat through painstaking meetings, discussing strategies and tactics, establishing democratic practices of decision making, building a membership base, and forging consensus on what politics to put forth publicly, Mckesson took a different path. With the exception of his short-lived and ill-fated Baltimore mayoral bid, it appears Mckesson has worked with a small team and concentrated largely on his web-based Campaign Zero police reform project and other social media activity. He also has a penchant for befriending celebrities. Mckesson once famously made the hyperbolic remark that "Twitter is the revolution."[9]

A more skeptical view of social media is articulated by Dream Defenders cofounder Phillip Agnew. At a large Black radicalism conference at Temple University in early 2016, Agnew gave a talk provocatively challenging the often-unquestioned role of social media in movement work.[10] This was after he and his Dream Defenders comrades took a temporary self-imposed hiatus, or "blackout" as they called it, from Twitter and Facebook. In the Temple speech, Agnew offered a harsh critique of social media as "an arena where unchecked hate, dominance, farce, and individualism now flourish," pointing out that social media often inflates egos, promotes individualism, and distracts from the hard work of face-to-face organizing.[11] In the final analysis, and Agnew's wise warnings notwithstanding, social media has been a critical and important tool for publicity and for creating a forum for debate and politicization. Overreliance on it, or assuming it can perform political miracles, is, however, misguided.

"WE YOUNG, WE STRONG, WE GONNA FIGHT FOR OUR FREEDOM ALL NIGHT LONG"

Chanted by many BLMM/M4BL protesters, the slogan in the above heading reflects the youth-centered character of the movement. While courageous and passionate young people have been at the cutting edge of every successful social and revolutionary movement throughout time, organizers and observers have to be careful about fetishizing "youth" as a political category. To be young is a phase of life, not a political status. There are radical, liberal, and conservative youth. And conversely, there are radical elders. When veteran civil rights spokesperson and media personality Reverend Al Sharpton encountered a hostile response from young Ferguson activists, and was confronted at his own rally in Washington, DC, in December 2014 by young activists from Ferguson, who insisted he did not represent them, the reason was not primarily his age. He was confronted, according to many Ferguson activists, because he was perceived as politically arrogant, opportunistic, and out of step with the politics of the day. In contrast, when radical feminist, socialist, and prison abolitionist Angela Y. Davis, eleven years Sharpton's senior, went to Ferguson during the height of the Ferguson demonstrations, she was warmly embraced: "She did not come at us the same way [that Sharpton did].," according to one young St. Louis activist. She was not trying to "scold and mold us."[12]

Similarly, sixty-five-year-old Jamala Rogers of Organization for Black Struggle; Makani Themba, the sixty-something former director of the Praxis Project; Linda Burnham of the National Domestic Workers Alliance; and legendary Black feminists Barbara Smith and Beverly Guy-Sheftall all have been accepted as trusted advisors and participants in this phase of struggle, as has

Cathy Cohen. A scholar-activist in her fifties, Cohen first conceived of and jumpstarted the formation that later evolved into BYP100, and she continues to work closely with the group. Robin D.G. Kelley, who is in his fifties, and I, now in my early sixties, continue to work closely with organizations in the BLMM/M4BL constellation. In the words of BYP100 leader Charlene Carruthers, most of the disagreements within the movement "are along the lines of ideology, not necessarily age."[13] That said, the optimism, energy, fervor, and fearlessness of youth, when harnessed to rigorous analysis and radical politics, are virtually unstoppable.

Young people in BLMM/M4BL, from Ferguson youth in Lost Voices to the more tightly organized BYP100, have embodied passion and determination that many observers have found awe inspiring. These young activists, standing toe to toe with police during tense demonstrations; refusing to obey orders from a militarized Ferguson police force; chanting brazenly, "Whose streets? Our streets!" and "Back up. Back up. We want our freedom, freedom. Racist-ass cops, we don't need 'em, need 'em," all represent a direct challenge to the legitimacy of violent state power as it currently exists. They are not recycling 1960s chants and songs but are rather employing bold new ones. They are a new generation claiming its voice of defiance, while at the same time holding onto a sense of history. Another popular chant that honors movement veterans and elders starts with "What side are you on, my people, what side are you on?" It continues, "Ella Baker was a freedom fighter, she taught us how to fight. We gonna fight all day and night until we get it right."

Both Ella Baker and Assata Shakur have been powerful symbols and inspirations for many of the BLMM/M4BL activists, especially BYP100. The group's 2017 national membership meeting in New Orleans embraced a quote by Ella Baker as its theme:

"We who believe in freedom [cannot rest]." T-shirts emblazoned with Baker's image were also widely distributed, and Baker is quoted widely in movement literature and speeches, especially her insistence that "strong people don't need a strong leader."

Led by the charismatic Atlanta-based organizer Mary Hooks of Southerners on New Ground, many movement gatherings end with the following statement, again emphasizing intergenerational ties: "The Mandate for Black people in this time is to avenge the suffering of our ancestors, to earn the respect of future generations, and to be willing to be transformed in the service of the work."[14] Hooks recites it with soul-stirring conviction, linking the contemporary movement both to history and to the future.

BLACK FEMINIST INFLUENCES

This generation of activists has been profoundly influenced directly and indirectly by the radical Black Feminist tradition that emerged in the 1970s, transmitted through books, poetry, images, personal relationships, and shared political spaces. This tradition, holistic, intersectional, radical, and inclusive, recognizes that the personal is political, and the political is profoundly personal.

Black feminist politics, language, and sensibilities are palpable throughout BLMM/M4BL movement circles. Some of these activists were feminists well before they became part of this phase of struggle, and others were exposed to new ideas, finding old ways of thinking challenged by the processes of struggle. "Assata Taught Us," a popular slogan on T-shirts worn by BLMM/M4BL organizers, refers to Black Liberation Army leader, former political prisoner, and political exile Assata Shakur, a strong woman who defied gender conventions in her leadership role in the Black Liberation Army in the 1970s. In a media interview, protest leader

Ashley Yates recalls coming up with the idea to use the term while sitting in a coffee shop in Ferguson and thinking about ways to capture the spirit of the uprising.[15] What better symbol than a militant Black woman who defied the odds to free herself from prison, as Shakur did before seeking exile in Cuba.

When asked which authors most impacted their evolving political edification, many leaders of BLMM/M4BL cited bell hooks, Angela Davis, Audre Lorde, Paula Giddings, Barbara Smith, Beth Richie, Cathy Cohen, Beverly Guy-Sheftall, myself (my book on Ella Baker), and finally fiction writer Toni Morrison, because of her creation of complex and self-determining female characters.[16] These were the intellectual building blocks of their collective consciousness, augmented by their own lived experiences and the wisdom of grandmothers, mothers, and aunties, who never wrote books but whose understanding of the complicated world ensured survival and inspired critical resistance.

How do these Black feminist politics show up in practice? The first line of Dream Defenders' vision statement reads as follows: "We believe that our liberation necessitates the destruction of the political and economic systems of Capitalism and Imperialism as well as Patriarchy." One of BYP100's fundamental principles is that they organize through "a black queer feminist lens," and are fighting for a "black queer feminist future." Similarly, BLMGN's work is informed by Black feminist politics and a dedication to the inclusion of LGBTQIA folk. And M4BL's tour de force policy document, the "Vision for Black Lives," highlights gender, class, citizenship, settler colonialism, sexuality, and environment, echoing the ethos of radical Black feminists' radically holistic politics on every page.[17]

The feminist organizers who launched and have led the BLMM/M4BL campaigns for the past four years have also wrestled with an obvious dilemma: the most highly publicized victims of police violence during this time, and in terms of dominant narratives, have been male. That is not because Black women have somehow been sheltered or exempted from such violence, as Andrea Ritchie's 2017 book, *Invisible No More*, graphically illustrates.[18] So Black feminist organizers have focused on the cases of women like Marissa Alexander, Sandra Bland, Rekia Boyd, Mya Hall, and Ayanna Stanley, while simultaneously supporting the high-profile cases of male victims. A Detroit-based filmmaker, feminist activist, cultural critic, and BLMM/M4BL supporter, dream hampton, directed and produced a powerful documentary that sought to expand who we see as victims of state violence, and even how we define the parameters of that violence. The film, *Treasure: From Tragedy to Trans Justice, Mapping a Detroit Story,* chronicles the life and murder of transgender teenager Shelley "Treasure" Hilliard. hampton is one of a number of artists who have contributed their talents to further the aims of #SAYHERNAME and of BLMM/M4BL in general.

In spring 2015, critical race theorist, legal scholar, and feminist Kimberlé Crenshaw and her African American Policy Forum, in collaboration with Andrea Ritchie and with Rachel Anspach, Rachel Gilmer, and Luke Harris, issued "Say Her Name: Resisting Police Brutality against Black Women," a report that documented hundreds of cases of police violence against Black women, many of which had gone virtually unnoticed by the media. The authors also offered statistics and a narrative frame that illuminate the contexts in which police violence against Black women often occurs. This was an outgrowth of the ongoing efforts by Crenshaw, Ritchie, and others to draw attention to the bias against, and invisibilization of, Black women and girls. In some ways the campaign can be traced back to feminist responses to President Obama's My Brother's Keeper initiative. In addition to Crenshaw, journalist and political scientist Melissa Harris-Perry also used her network and platform to amplify the demand for more federal attention to the needs of Black women and girls in the president's agenda, eventually organizing a historic conference at the White House on this very subject.

In 2014, a group of activists led by Crenshaw came together to launch "Why We Can't Wait," a campaign to demand expansion of Obama's My Brother's Keeper's effort to include women and girls, and later to put forward a media campaign called "Black Girls Matter." According to Gilmer, and simply put, "We argued that you cannot have a program that elevates the needs of Black men, without elevating the needs of the women who raise them and the sisters they grow up with."[19] Kimberlé Crenshaw's work demanded not only resources but protection from violence for Black women and girls as well. With a powerful TED talk seen by tens of thousands of viewers, in which she told some of the stories behind the statistics, Crenshaw helped to make the narrative of Black women and police violence real for a large audience. By early May 2015, much research had gone into the violence report, but a release date had not yet been set. The authors had decided on a title, though. It was *Say Her Name,* an obvious reference to the many nameless Black women killed by police or victimized by other forms of state violence.

In parallel time, a group of Chicago-based activists had been working to publicize the case of Rekia Boyd after the 2015 acquittal of Dante Servin, the Chicago cop who fatally shot her in 2012. BYP100 was the main catalyst for this effort, viewing it as part of a larger effort to push back against the narrative about police violence that focused almost solely on men. They had marched, chanted, and cried in response to the cases of Michael Brown,

Trayvon Martin, Philando Castile, and others, but they knew those incidents were only half the story. Rekia Boyd's case, for example, told a different story, and the young feminist activists in BYP100, along with the Chicago-based Project NIA, Black Lives Matter Chicago (BLM-Chi), Assata's Daughters, and other groups, were determined to disseminate her story, along with those of women like her, as widely as possible.

BYP100, joined with the groups Ferguson Action and BLMGN, issued a call for a day of action on May 21, 2015, to remember women and girls who had been victims of violence. Dozens of cities, from Memphis to Atlanta, to San Francisco, to Chicago, to New York, agreed to participate. The Movement for Black Lives organizers were recruited to help cast a wider net and pull in other activists around the country, while BYP100 chapters also planned local actions.

When the *Say Her Name* authors learned of the day of action being planned, Andrea Ritchie reached out to Carruthers of BYP100 to see if coordinating the release of the report with the May 21 events would be helpful. Carruthers agreed, and the report was issued on May 20, giving momentum to the protests. The African American Policy Forum had its own vigil in New York's Union Square the night the report was released, with Crenshaw, feminist activist and playwright Eve Ensler, and some of the families of slain women on the program.

On May 21, BYP100 held an emotional rally in New York City, and Movement for Black Lives affiliates rallied, mourned, engaged in rituals of remembrance, and disrupted business as usual in some twenty cities to draw attention to the myriad forms of state violence that impact Black women and girls. They fused their efforts with the African American Policy Forum–derived banner, #SAYHERNAME. They also used the hashtags

#JusticeforRekia and #Blackwomenmatter. In San Francisco, over a dozen Black women bared their breasts in a dramatic protest to demand attention to both the objectification of Black women's bodies and the harm done to those bodies. With the protesters linking arms to block traffic in San Francisco's busy financial district, the San Francisco protest was by far the most visually and viscerally impactful.

#SAYHERNAME was not just an event, it was part of an ongoing effort to expose the links between state violence and sexual violence. Another critical case that captured the attention of feminists working against gender-based state violence was that of Oklahoma police officer Daniel Holtzclaw, who had assaulted, raped, and/or sodomized thirteen Black women while they were in his custody. This case was both outrageous and complicated. Outrageous because there were so many women involved, the abuse was so egregious, and the incidents had occurred over an extended period of time. Complicated because most of the women had criminal records, past drug addictions, and a collective history of arrests. The question was, would they be believed? A team of progressive lawyers working with grassroots activists set about making the legal case and publicizing the women's stories to make them legible and sympathetic to the public. One of those leaders was Grace Franklin, cofounder of the OKC Artists for Justice. The net result was a conviction on thirteen of the thirty-six charges, and an unprecedented 263-year prison sentence for Holtzclaw.[20] While some activists definitely called for a long prison sentence for Holtzclaw, abolitionists were ambivalent. Even in this heinous case, some BLMM/M4BL organizers argued not for prison time but for attention to the needs of the survivors and some assurances that the offender would be stripped of his power and monitored to prevent future abuses. At the same time, no one protested the sentence, and many applauded it.

Of the dozens of women shot, beaten, and brutalized by law enforcement over the past few years, two cases stand out, because organizers built campaigns that made what would otherwise have been invisible visible. One is that of Sandra Bland, the woman who was pulled over by a local police officer in Texas for allegedly changing lanes without using her turn signal and who ended up dead in her jail cell a short time later. The video of Bland's rough and unnecessary arrest for a minor traffic violation went viral after the twenty-eight-year-old's suspicious death in custody was deemed a suicide. As Black feminist activists and others protested Bland's death, her name began to appear everywhere—on Twitter and in speeches and articles about police violence. Her family's vigilance (especially that of her sister) helped to keep a spotlight on the case. Ultimately no one was charged in her death, but the vivid details of her case drew attention to the issue of police violence and harassment of Black women.[21] The second standout case was that of Rekia Boyd, which will be discussed in a later chapter. It was yet another example of applied Black feminist and Black feminist abolitionist politics. Boyd was killed, and Chicago activists led a campaign to have the off-duty police officer who killed her fired. The persistence and volume of the grassroots "Justice for Rekia" movement took Boyd's case from obscurity to the national spotlight.

ABOLITION, ACCOUNTABILITY, AND HEALING

Political work is not done by angels or robots but by people—complicated and beautifully imperfect human beings, all of whom have been socialized in a hetero-patriarchal capitalist society. In the scholarship on other social movements, and in the memoirs of many participants, we see how competition, ego, sexism, homophobia, and even interpersonal violence have plagued past movements. These dynamics were not predominant in most movements, but they were present. BLMM/M4BL is no exception. But the ways in which organizers have tried to deal with these internal challenges are perhaps exceptional and hopeful. Jamala Rogers underscores the importance of movement healing when she writes, "And what of redemption? When wrongdoing and harm has been acknowledged by those in our movement, there's rarely a healing process that takes into full account both accountability and personal salvation. Restorative justice has a vital place in our movement, not just in the corrupt courts system."[22] This abolitionist/restorative justice impulse travels throughout the BLMM/ M4BL circuit of organizations and is reflected in speeches, websites, movement documents, and practice.

One particularly complicated case of sexual impropriety, played out in social and mainstream print media in Chicago, tested the movement's commitment to accountability and restorative justice. A prominent, charismatic, and well-respected young cisgender male organizer with BYP100 was accused of sexual assault. The incident had happened years before, when the activist was a teenager, and involved an acquaintance, unwanted sexual advances, and sexual touching without consent. The young woman had carried this experience with her and was retraumatized when she saw the person who had violated her raised up as a hero in the movement. Not invested in the police or punishment as a solution, she instead turned to the movement, writing an open letter telling her story.

BYP100 defines itself as a Black feminist organization, and it was quick to respond. The organization invited Mariame Kaba, a longtime activist and trusted local facilitator and restorative justice/transformative justice practitioner, to help. With her guidance, they hoped to put in place a healing and restorative process that centered on the young woman's concerns. The male member was suspended from leadership, and a team began working on the case to get both parties to agree to a process of healing and restitution. The process extended over at least an eighteen-month period. It was an arduous, messy, and time-consuming process, but BYP100 managed to see it through.[23] BYP100 dealt similarly with several other cases that were not as high profile but also had to do with displays of what they describe as "toxic masculinity." BYP100 has created a Healing and Safety Council, with the input of scholar, activist, and BYP100 member Kai Green and others, and has institutionalized policies to address various transgressions. Similarly, BLMGN has a full-time staff person devoted exclusively to healing justice.

This is one way that contemporary activists are sharper and more principled in their handling of allegations of sexism and sexual assault, and the stresses and strains that come with political organizing, than previous generations. Even the survivor who was not a member of BYP100 herself felt positive about the process: "I'm very impressed that BYP is willing to take the time to go through the accountability process," she observed.[24]

During my research on Ella Baker, I remember vividly the stories women in the civil rights movement told me about sexual harassment and assault in movement circles in the 1960s. At that time, few women dared to report such instances except to close girlfriends. And some still whispered about it decades later. They feared that their revelations might be used against movement organizations and leaders by those who wanted to discredit the work. The accusation of "airing dirty laundry" as a silencing tactic is documented in Aishah Simmons's *NO!*, a powerful documentary about rape in the Black community, and in Danielle McGuire's powerful book *At the Dark End of the Street*.[25]

More recently, Anita Hill made the very credible claim in 1991 that US Supreme Court nominee Clarence Thomas had sexually harassed her years before when she worked for him. She fought an uphill battle to be believed. Her case sparked the formation of another important organizational antecedent to BLMM/M4BL, cofounded by Elsa Barkley Brown, Deborah King, and myself: African American Women in Defense of Ourselves, a Black women's solidarity campaign, raised fifty thousand dollars and composed a statement, signed by sixteen hundred Black women. Published in the *New York Times* and in several African American weeklies, the statement insisted that Hill be believed and her allegations be taken seriously. The statement also outlined the complex intersection of race, class, gender, and sexuality in the lives of Black women. Fast-forward twenty-five years. While sexual harassment and assault are still real within the Black community and society at large, at least social movement organizations have mechanisms and a commitment to respond.

Internal movement struggles and tensions are real, but so are concerted efforts to foster fairness and a sense of political community without glossing over issues of politics, power, and privilege. Expert and committed facilitators like Adrienne Maree Brown from Detroit; Makani Temba from Jackson, Mississippi, and Detroit; Ayoka Turner and Ntanya Lee from Oakland; and Denise Perry from Miami have guided many of these organizations and coalitions through difficult processes of decision making and conflict resolution. This is a necessary and healthy component of movement-building. Restorative justice practitioners like Mariame Kaba and Black healers like the women and femmes in the Harriet's Apothecary health and healing collective, founded by Adaku Utah in 2014, have been tremendous resources for BLMM/M4BL organizers and organizations.[26]

Both intracommunal violence (violence within the Black community) and state violence against transgender and gender-nonconforming Black people have also been issues around which BLMM/ M4BL groups and individuals have organized, making visible some of the most vulnerable members of our communities and confronting homophobia and transphobia in the process. The work of transgender activist Elle Hearn, former BLMGN staff person and founder of the Marsha P. Johnson Institute; the advocacy and service work of Brave Space Alliance, led by LaSaia Wade, a Black trans woman in Chicago and member of BLM-CHI; and the efforts of Georgia-based queer transgender activist Raquel Willis, national coordinator for the Transgender Law Center, are but three examples of this work by individuals who are either part of or loosely affiliated with BLMM/M4BL. Another group in the BLMM/M4BL orbit whose work warrants mention is Freedom Inc. in Madison. Led by queer and gender-nonconforming activist M. Adams, the group brings together Black and Southeast Asian survivors of violence, especially gender and sexual violence, to build new leadership and to organize collaboratively. Freedom Inc.'s "Hands Off Black Womyn" campaign successfully fought for the release of a number of Black people who were incarcerated because they were gender nonconforming, sex workers, or defending themselves against sexual or domestic violence.

Another critically important campaign that reflects the intersectional feminist politics of the movement is the work of the queer, Southern-based racial and economic justice group Southerners on New Ground (SONG) to advance the efforts to end cash bail. People who have been charged with a crime and are awaiting trial—in other words, people who are presumed innocent, since they have not been convicted of anything—languish in jails around the country because they are too poor to make bail and be released until their trial dates. Many of these people are women, and many of these women are mothers. SONG contributed mightily to the campaign to end cash bail through its Black Mama's Bail Out on Mother's Day 2017. Through its partnership with preexisting bail reform groups, SONG has enabled the release of dozens of women, reuniting them with their families and children.[27] SONG's vision, and the inspirational leadership of its codirector Mary Hooks, has propelled this work forward and made explicit the links between gender justice, racial justice, the injustice of sexual oppression, and the injustice of the jail and prison industries.

CLASS POLITICS AND MONEY

> Capitalism with Black in front of it won't liberate our people.
>
> Charlene Carruthers

By centering poor, marginalized, and formerly incarcerated sectors of the Black community, in addition to LGBTQIA folks, BLMM/M4BL inescapably positions itself in opposition to neoliberal racial capitalism, though of course opposition to the extreme injustices of capitalism does not necessarily mean endorsement of a system-wide overhaul.[28] The nuances of the movement's positions on class and capitalism, which have been a subject of internal discussion and debate, continue to evolve.

While some have argued that Black businesses and Black capitalism should be part of a strategy for Black liberation, my view is that the majority consensus within BLMM/M4BL circles builds on Cedric Robinson's assessment of racial capitalism as one of the foundations of Black social and economic oppression.[29] The "Vision for Black Lives" statement states explicitly, "We stand in solidarity with our international family against the ravages of global capitalism," and outlines a platform agenda that concentrates on issues most impacting poor and working-class Black folk.[30] The vision statement, the most developed policy statement of the movement, includes a condemnation of cash bail, support for increasing the minimum wage, a defense of labor unions, support of immigrant workers, condemnation of student debt, and a call for free education, among its many socialist-leaning economic justice proposals. BYP100's "Agenda to Build Black Futures" policy document opens with the following: "America's economic system has systematically failed Black communities."[31]

The political education agendas of BYP100, Dream Defenders, and M4BL overall have included readings and discussions about the history and nature of racial capitalism. In 2017, members of M4BL participated in workshops/think tanks in Chicago with presentations by Black Left scholars and writers, including Donna Murch, Lester Spence, Leith Mullings, Cornel West, Beverly Guy-Sheftall, Robin D.G. Kelley, Michael Dawson, and myself. Earlier national BLMM/M4BL gatherings featured discussions of racial capitalism and included a range of Black Left thinkers, including Ruth Wilson Gilmore, Cathy Cohen, Beth Richie, Brittany Cooper, and Kali Akuno, codirector of Cooperation Jackson, a network of Mississippi-based cooperatives. A handful of organizers working on M4BL are also members or supporters of socialist organizations, most notably Freedom Road Socialist Organization, the newly formed LeftRoots, and the International Socialist Organization. Radical anticapitalist thinkers within

BLMM/M4BL like James Hayes, formerly of the Ohio Student Association, have organized various retreats and international discussions about race, Marxism, and social change.

Finally, I have been struck by the personal and family stories of many core organizers in the BLMM/M4BL network. Some of these stories have been shared in confidence, so I will not mention them by name, but BLMGN cofounder Patrisse Khan-Cullors[32] talks openly about her family's experiences with poverty, the criminal justice system, and the police in her public interviews and writings.[33] Other key organizers have parents or siblings who are currently or were formerly incarcerated. Some have experienced brief bouts of homelessness and longer periods of unemployment. Others still are struggling single parents trying to make ends meet and change the world at the same time. They are not, as I once overheard someone say disparagingly, "a bunch of Black college kids." Students and college-trained professionals are involved, but many others come from working-class backgrounds and others still live in Black working-class and poor communities. In other words, they understand, as several pieces of literature have asserted, that racial justice is economic justice and vice versa.

The inescapable tension about money is another aspect of the class dynamics within BLMM/M4BL that warrants mention. Many of the new BLMM/M4BL organizations are either non-profits with 501(c)(3) tax-exempt status or have fiscal sponsors that allow them to receive grants and donations, hire staff, pay for travel, rent space, and print literature. Funding allows organizers to work full-time, perhaps with greater focus and efficiency. It also creates new problems and vulnerabilities. Even with the best intentions, there is competition between organizations and, not surprisingly, tension between the objectives of funders and the political goals of organizations. To their great credit, BLMM/M4BL leaders took the unusual step of setting up a resources table to try to more equitably distribute and reallocate funds that were being directed toward the movement, often in an unbalanced way. For the most part, tensions over resources have been managed or muted. However, sometimes conflicts about money and resources bubble up to the surface. Ferguson was one example of this.

The greater Ferguson area was for nearly a year the epicenter of Black resistance to police-based state violence. Young people who had never been involved in political actions before were thrust into the spotlight. Decisions were made in the heat of battle. And the battles were intense. Amid teargas and tanks, street protestors continued to come out to rally, march, chant, and demand action. Many people felt they were in a war zone, viewing themselves as warriors for a just cause. Even though no deaths were attributed directly to the Ferguson uprising, the human toll was high. People lost their jobs, suffered numerous arrests and injuries, endured threats, and experienced mental and physical fatigue. At least one young activist was sentenced to serious jail time.

As Ferguson garnered national and international attention, outside supporters began to funnel money and resources into the area. The money helped and, in some unintentional ways, it also hurt. According to local St. Louis organizers, few, if any, Black organizations in Ferguson were willing and able to accept this volume of donations. So the progressive but predominantly white group Missourians Organizing for Reform and Empowerment (MORE) agreed to serve that function, working in tandem with the long-established Organization for Black Struggle. Some activists were upset when they got wind of the money sitting in MORE's bank account. They felt they should have a say in how the money was distributed, but there was not an over-arching movement infrastructure that everyone had agreed to that could have resolved such a dispute, even though a decision-making plan was being established. A bit of chaos ensued.

Things came to a head on May 14, 2015, when seventeen Black activists who had been on the streets of Ferguson week after week occupied the offices of MORE and demanded that the staff write them seventeen checks dividing up the funds. Under pressure, the white executive director did just that and was harshly criticized by Organization for Black Struggle leaders and others after the fact. Jamala Rogers wrote bluntly, "The shake-down pretty much cleaned out a bank account designed to support movement activities."[34] Rogers is a seasoned activist, who long ago opted to forego what might have been a more comfortable and lucrative career in favor of a life in disciplined struggle and movement work. She undoubtedly made sacrifices to do so. She was appalled by what she viewed as self-serving strong-arm tactics by a handful of individuals to obtain what were intended to be movement resources.

The inexperienced activists who occupied MORE's offices, on the other hand, felt they were taking blows, making sacrifices, and experiencing threatened evictions and job losses. They felt their actions had, in part, inspired the funds flowing into Ferguson and so they deserved some financial relief. They created the hashtag #cutthecheck to underscore their demands and rally supporters on social media. This was a dramatic example of confrontation over resources, but more subtle tensions exist in every movement that seeks outside funding.

The #cutthecheck episode also revealed deep class and generational divides. Older activists came of age politically when the expectation of "getting paid" was nonexistent. Today's activists see their peers and some middle-class elders earning a comfortable income, in some cases, by doing various forms of community organizing. Also, when broad-based movements are at their peak, they bring together people with very different levels of class privilege. Folks who are barely getting by on poverty-level wages or below are in a coalition that includes professionals with college degrees and lucrative salaries. This is a recipe for some level of tension.

The six themes and areas of tension described in this chapter offer a small glimpse into the complex inner workings of the BLMM/M4BL network, with layered dynamics that are very much in flux, and reflective of politics and collective values that are still evolving.

SIX

Backlash and a Price

The internal challenges faced by leaders of the Black Lives Matter Movement and Movement for Black Lives (BLMM/M4BL) notwithstanding, the bigger fight that the movement has taken on is with oppositional forces, those who want to preserve some version of the status quo and the existing racialized hierarchies of power. Movements for change are sustained mobilizations and campaigns in response to oppressive and unjust conditions. But for every action there is a reaction, and the backlash against BLMM/M4BL has been steady and formidable. That the movement has held its ground, expanded, and matured under pressure is quite a feat. In 2017, five years after Trayvon Martin was murdered and three years after Michael Brown was killed in Ferguson, BLMM/M4BL's work continues to grow in interesting and palpable ways but not without costs and setbacks.

Hundreds were arrested in the streets of Ferguson and Baltimore, and hundreds more were teargassed, roughed up, and shot at with rubber bullets. There were detentions, overnight arrests, and, in a few cases, serious criminal charges. Most protesters got off with misdemeanors or community service, or the charges were dropped. In some cities, however, prosecutors sought to teach activists a lesson. Random shootings of police officers by lone gunmen, who were unaffiliated with movement organizations but sometimes usurped the language and slogans of Black Lives Matter, were flash points. This only added to the growing attacks and criticisms of BLMM/M4BL by politicians and media pundits. The height of this backlash came in July 2016, when five Dallas police officers were ambushed and killed by a single Black gunman, and conservatives tried to blame Black Lives Matter, even in one case labeling it a "terrorist" movement.[1] Social media attacks were even more vicious, and some activists feared for their safety amid threats of retribution for something they had no hand in.

Dallas was not the beginning of the backlash against BLMM/M4BL, however. In December 2014, Minnesota Black Lives Matter organizers shut down the Mall of America, drawing a connection between rampant consumerism and the lack of resources and rights in poor Black communities. According to the group's Facebook post, "Thousands of people stood together, refused to be intimidated, and disrupted business as usual on the busiest shopping day of the year at the biggest mall in the country. As long as innocent Black and brown lives are disrupted by police without consequence, we cannot go about business as usual."[2] As with many actions and campaigns of BLMM/M4BL groups, the Minnesota activists were making a political statement that linked economics and state violence.

Mall of America protesters filled the mall rotunda and then staged die-ins in the mall corridors. Eventually the police made about two dozen arrests. What came next was an attempt to levy harsh penalties against those arrested in order to deter any future protesters who would dare to disrupt the flow of commerce. Not only were protesters charged with disorderly conduct and other misdemeanors, but the prosecutor also asked that they be forced to pay restitution for the cost of police coverage and even for the businesses' loss of revenue. Ultimately the charges were dropped and no restitution was paid, but the hefty threat was unheard of and a flagrant gesture of intimidation.

That was not the end of the story in Minnesota. A year later, BLMGN activists there experienced an especially violent assault. Five Black Lives Matter protesters, who were maintaining an encampment outside a police station in north Minneapolis to protest the police shooting of Jamar Clark, themselves became shooting victims. Fortunately, all of those injured recovered. The shooting occurred in November 2015, when four masked men came to taunt, disrupt, and eventually violently attack the BLMGN group.[3] Four men were charged and at least one man was convicted of felonious assault. This attack underscored the vulnerability of activists who stage high-profile public actions and those who organize them.

One of the most prominent cases of mass arrest and trial of BLMM/M4BL organizers involved a group of Bay Area activists known as the Black Friday 14, which included #BlackLivesMatter cofounder Alicia Garza. In November 2014, they chained themselves to a BART train in Oakland on Black Friday, disrupting the nation's fifth-busiest rapid transit system for several hours in order to protest both violence and heavy-handed policing by BART cops, as well as transit-related gentrification and displacement of working Black residents of West Oakland.[4] The case of the Black Friday 14 dragged on for an entire year, until the charges were finally dropped after a sustained campaign to free them.[5] Veteran radical lawyer and black Oakland activist Walter Riley defended the group, and a national defense campaign drew attention to the case.

Two of the harshest and most punitive outcomes suffered by anti–police violence protesters in this period were those of young Josh Williams in Ferguson, and twenty-eight-year-old Jasmine Abdullah Richards in California. Williams was a mainstay of the Ferguson uprising in 2014. He rallied at City Hall, linked arms in protest marches with celebrities, spoke at press conferences, defied curfew, and one night in the thick of the fray threw a match into a trash receptacle outside a QuikTrip in the nearby town of Berkeley, Missouri. The Berkeley protests were a response to yet another murder of an unarmed, local Black teenager—Antonio Martin. Williams's act, caught on video camera, changed his life forever. The authorities decided to make an example of him. Even though no one was injured, and the fire was put out before it did very much damage, the prosecutor called for a brutally stiff sentence. The judge settled on eight years.[6] This is a harsh punishment for a teenager who had lashed out at property, not people. Ferguson organizers raised money for Williams's legal defense and packed the courtroom for this sentencing, but the final outcome was a major blow that drew tears months later as local activists Elizabeth Vega and Nabeegah Azeri remembered Josh and what happened to him.[7]

In August 2015, Jasmine Abdullah Richards, a twenty-eight-year-old Black, female BLMGN organizer, was arrested in Pasadena, California, for allegedly attempting to "de-arrest" a fellow protestor demonstrating at a local park. On June 2, 2016, she was convicted of the outrageous charge of "felony lynching,"[8] which is a nearly obsolete 1930s law originally directed at white vigilantes. In her case, she was accused of violating a part of the law that refers to any effort to take a person out of police custody—what lynch mobs did before stringing up Black victims, who were denied trial, due process, or other such protections. Black Lives Matter Los Angeles organizer and professor Melina Abdullah expressed the indignation that many felt: "So it's really disgusting and ironic that she's charged and convicted with felony lynching, when the real lynching that's carried out is done in the same way it was carried out in the late nineteenth, early twentieth century, where it's supposed to punish those who dare to rise up against a system."[9]

Richards faced up to four years in prison but ultimately received a ninety-day sentence followed by three years probation. Social media exploded in support of Richards, with Rosa Clemente tweeting, "She is the first political prisoner of BLM."[10] Racist responses on Twitter followed in predictable fashion. The following is typical: "Don't free, send her to the gas chamber with all the other racist niggers in blm."[11] While Jasmine Abdullah Richards was able to escape a longer sentence, she still carries a felony conviction and all the restrictions that come with it. The last time I saw her at a BLM national gathering, she was still traumatized and distraught by the entire ordeal.

The largest wave of backlash was perhaps during the 2016 presidential campaign of Donald Trump. Large crowds, overwhelmingly, if not all, white gathered to hear Trump belittle Mexicans, Muslims, and women. And of course Trump revealed his own anti-Black racism as early as 2008, when he railed that the United States' first Black president was likely not born in the United States and demanded Obama produce his birth certificate, fueling the so-called birther movement against the new president.[12]

BLMM/M4BL activists, like thousands of Americans, protested at Trump rallies around the country. Many were singled out for vitriolic comments and even physical attacks. As Carol

Anderson notes in her 2016 book, *White Rage,* the mobilization and deployment of white anger at Black progress (or what is perceived as Black progress) and Black self-defense has been a mainstay of white supremacist structures and practices since slavery and has emboldened a significant sector of Trump's followers.[13] In addition to making racist and xenophobic remarks—calling Black protesters "monkeys," and telling them to "go back to Africa"[14]—some Trump supporters even physically assaulted Black protesters, who were invariably outnumbered.[15]

Fox News and other conservative media outlets have targeted Black Lives Matter for some pretty vicious attacks as well. As one article outlines it, "In 2015, Fox News' three primetime hosts engaged in a smear campaign against the Black Lives Matter movement, fear mongering about the alleged threat they pose to law and order and hyping racist canards aimed at discrediting the movement's calls for justice." Fox News' now-ousted demagogue Bill O'Reilly labeled Black Lives Matter a "hate group."[16] And in 2017 the FBI's counterterrorism division declared so-called *Black Identity Extremists,* a new, awkward, and vague term, to be a violent threat to national security.[17] BLMGN, its founders, and the dozen or so local and national groups that collectively form M4BL routinely receive threats, hate mail, and nasty attacks by social media trolls.

In most cases, movement organizers are concerned about external threats, but there are internal and deeply personal threats as well. On a cold February day in 2016, a young spoken-word poet, organizer, and leader of the Ohio Student Association, an affiliate of the Movement for Black Lives, stood on the steps of the Ohio Statehouse in Columbus, in the shadows of its Greek Revival pillars and statues of US political heroes, and shot himself to death. His name was MarShawn McCarrel, and he was only twenty-three years old. He had suffered from depression, but his friends and fellow activists also speculated that arrests, death threats, and the emotional stress related to a movement steeped in protesting and reimagining the death of others may have taken a toll. After McCarrel's tragic suicide, others in the movement spoke openly about the emotional and psychological pressures of movement work.[18] Nearly two years after this tragedy, Opal Tometi confided that she still thought of and mourned the loss of MarShawn.[19]

It is significant that many in the movement have embraced a very powerful quote from Assata Shakur that reverberated through many street demonstrations: "It is our duty to fight for our freedom. It is our duty to win. We must love each other and protect each other. We have nothing to lose but our chains."[20] Some young movement activists have tattooed the quote on their bodies. The militant determination embodied in this quote is clear. What is equally important in this particular quote is the ethos of love and shared commitment, not only to political ideals, but also to one another.

SEVEN

A View from the Local

Chicago's Fighting Spirit

To understand the dynamics of BLMM/M4BL, we have to look beyond the national to the local. A commonly repeated truth is that "all politics are local," meaning that national movements and campaigns are built upon the concrete work performed on the local level.[1] While it is beyond the scope of this project to cover all the vibrant local struggles out there, I will take Chicago as a case study, even though it is by no means typical.

Chicago has been the site of intense resistance to racist state violence for decades. The 1969 police murder of twenty-one-year-old Illinois Black Panther Party leader Fred Hampton is still remembered bitterly in the city's African American community. Hampton was a youth leader in the National Association for the Advancement of Colored People and later joined the Illinois Black Panther Party, rising in the ranks to become its chair. A charismatic organizer, he built bridges between the party and Chicago's Puerto Rican, Mexican, and poor white communities, in what he called a rainbow coalition. In an early-morning police raid on an apartment in Chicago's West Side on December 4, 1969, Hampton was shot and killed while his pregnant girlfriend lay in the bed next to him. Mark Clark, Hampton's comrade, was also killed in the infamous raid. Their murders were an outgrowth of the FBI's notorious COINTELPRO (counterintelligence program), which sought to subvert and destroy Black liberation organizations that the government deemed threatening. The FBI was willing to use almost any means to do so.[2]

Only a few years after Hampton's assassination, Area 2 police commander Jon Burge began what would become a decades-long practice of torture in the back room of the Chicago police station that he oversaw. Many African American men in Burge's custody on the city's South Side were coerced into giving false confessions—some of them ended up languishing for years on death row. A subgroup of them, dubbed "the Death Row Ten," refused to suffer in silence and began to organize from behind bars. They became strong and eloquent advocates for their own freedom. The men told their stories and pleaded for help, but for many years they were simply ignored.

It was only through a systematic campaign by activist groups and torture victims' families that the truth finally came to light. It was exposed that some victims were burned with lit cigarettes, others had plastic bags put over their heads, and some suffered electric shock to their genitals. It took a determined and protracted campaign to finally extract some modicum of justice. The Illinois Campaign to End the Death Penalty eventually got on board and was instrumental in mobilizing support specifically for the Death Row Ten. Some of the torture victims received reduced sentences, monetary settlements, and exonerations from the governor.

Torture survivors like Ronnie Kitchen, Anthony Holmes, Mark Clements, and Darrell Cannon told compelling and gut-wrenching stories of their experiences and became effective voices for the movement upon their release. In 2000, Republican governor George Ryan was persuaded to declare a moratorium on the death penalty in Illinois and commute the sentences of all 160 death row inmates, among them a number of Burge torture survivors.[3] I remember meeting Ronnie Kitchen at a welcome home party thrown by anti–death penalty activist Alice Kim a few days after his release. I was struck by the gentle humility of this man after all he had suffered.

Alice Kim, the daughter of Korean immigrants and raised in the suburbs of Chicago, was a key organizer in the Illinois Campaign to End the Death Penalty when Ronnie reached out to the group in 1998 with a letter proclaiming his innocence. She met Ronnie in 1999, when he was still on death row, and she took his mother, Louva Bell, to the Pontiac Correctional Center to visit. Weekly phone calls for nearly ten years anchored their deepening political friendship. With Louva by her side and a range of political groups, ranging from the International Socialist Organization to Reverend Jesse Jackson's Rainbow PUSH Coalition, Alice fought like hell to free Ronnie and the other Burge torture victims on Illinois's death row—all of them Black and all of them poor. Most were eventually released.[4]

The relentless campaign to free Ronnie and his fellow torture survivors involved numerous Chicago organizers, radical lawyers like Joey Mogul and Flint Taylor at the People's Law Offices, and members of the men's own families. By the time Burge's deeds were fully revealed, the statute of limitations had run out, which prevented his being prosecuted for his most heinous crimes. He was, however, ultimately convicted on the federal level on the secondary charge of perjury for lying to prosecutors about what he did. Phase 1 of the struggle was to expose the torture and free the survivors. Phase 2 was to hold those guilty of torture accountable. Phase 3 was to win some form of restitution for the survivors.

Finally, in May 2015, a broad-based community coalition was successful in getting the Chicago City Council to pass an unprecedented reparations ordinance on behalf of the torture survivors. Although this victory was limited, it was powerful in a number of respects. In addition to awarding a five-million dollar settlement to the remaining victims who had not been included in earlier lawsuits, it added the following forms of collective restitution: a unit in the Chicago Public Schools' curriculum that would teach students about this ugly chapter in Chicago's history; a public memorial to the victims of police torture; free tuition to Chicago's public colleges for the victims, their children, and their grandchildren; a counseling center for torture victims and their families; and priority access to many city services. This creative and far-reaching settlement was an important landmark in the struggle to hold police and city officials accountable and to reimagine what reparations demands might look like.[5] It also won changes that will have an impact beyond the torture victims and their families.

While as of this writing the reparations ordinance is perhaps the most high-profile victory of the struggle against police violence in Chicago, the story would be distorted were the decades of work by radical Black lawyer Standish Willis, who was suing the police and city for brutalizing its Black citizens as early as the 1980s, not mentioned. Through his work with the National Conference of Black Lawyers and his early affiliation with the People's Law Offices, Willis was a fierce fighter for police accountability. He met with people at their kitchen tables and in church basements to bolster the courage of litigants at a time when many were afraid to stand up to the police. I remember soon after I moved to

Chicago in 1991 accompanying Willis to meetings with community residents, where he gave people confidence that they could sue the police and actually win. Even when victims came out of custody with black eyes and bruises, many Black community residents were skeptical that they could obtain justice through the courts. Willis, working closely with the organization he cofounded, Black People against Police Torture, always insisted that a combination of community organizing and courtroom strategy would yield results. Many of his lawsuits were successful against the odds. His pioneering work elevated the consciousness and political will of the community, which contributed to the ultimate victory of the ordinance. These are some of the foundations of activism and resistance supporting the 2012–16 anti–police violence campaigns in Chicago.

Another case of police violence that captured the hearts and triggered the anger of Chicago activists is that of Dominique (Damo) Franklin Jr., who was Tased by police in May 2014 and died as a result. This case did not initially get much publicity. Damo, like many young Black men in Chicago, had experienced various run-ins with the police. On the night of his death, he had allegedly stolen some small items from a local store and was fleeing police, unarmed. Police Tased him twice while he was in motion. As he fell, he hit a pole, which caused a severe head injury, resulting in his death. Poets and community organizers Malcolm London and Ethan Viets-Vanlear were friends of Damo's. Ethan visited him in the hospital just before he died. The police involved were never charged.[6] His death was a catalyst for some of his friends to become more politically active.

Veteran organizer Mariame Kaba was the first to invite Damo's friends and others to a meeting in June 2014, where she proposed forming a delegation of young people of color to make a case against the Chicago Police Department and highlight Damo's death before the United Nation's Committee against Torture (UNCAT). The delegates, most of whom were under twenty-five years old at the time, included Ethan, Malcolm, and seven other young Chicago activists: Todd St. Hill, Breanna Champion, Asha Ransby-Sporn, Ric Wilson, Page May, and Monica Trinidad. Together they formed the We Charge Genocide delegation, echoing the 1951 international campaign that included Paul Robeson and drew attention to the heinous practice of lynching Black people in the US South by taking their cases to the UN.[7] After raising the needed funds, the young Chicagoans traveled to a UN meeting in Geneva, Switzerland, in November 2014 to render testimony on the pattern of police violence in Chicago's Black communities. They returned to an enthusiastic welcome from Chicago activists. The delegates presented a report on their trip to Geneva to a crowd of five hundred people at Roosevelt University.

In an unprecedented gesture, when issuing its final report, UNCAT explicitly cited the Chicago Police Department for its reckless use of Tasers and referenced Damo's death. Additionally, the report called on the City of Chicago to pass the reparations ordinance for Burge torture survivors. These were both victories for the We Charge Genocide delegation. In September 2017, the City of Chicago agreed to a two-hundred-thousand-dollar settlement with Damo's family, tacitly acknowledging that the officers were in the wrong when they Tased him.[8] We Charge Genocide, which turned into a sustained two-year effort, further galvanized the growing anti–police violence movement in the city, a movement deeply implicated in larger campaigns to expose economic injustice and other forms of state violence and to advocate for prison abolition and transformative justice practices. Importantly, the Chicago We Charge Genocide effort inspired Ferguson activists to raise money to send Michael Brown's parents and lawyer Justin Hansford to the United Nations in Geneva to make a similar case about the killing of Michael Brown.

Black feminists like Kaba did much of the behind-the-scenes work, strategizing, and planning that facilitated the We Charge Genocide delegation: political education, research for a well-documented report that was produced by the WCG collective, testimony, and mentoring of a new crop of bold young organizers. Jasson Perez, one of the founding members of BYP100, recalls that Mariame "had a profound impact on many of us and how we see our work.... But bigger than that, she was essential in establishing a Black feminist programmatic political orientation in all our work. She was the best example of how to practically enact a Black queer feminist politic at the policy and campaign level."[9] Kaba also helped publicize and organize around the Tiawanda Moore case. Moore, aged twenty, was a young Black woman charged with but acquitted of a felony for audiotaping two Chicago police officers, who were trying to dissuade her from filing a sexual assault complaint against one of their fellow officers. She was also the target of sexist attacks from the media for having once worked as a stripper, a fact that had nothing to do with her case.[10]

The case that really galvanized Chicago's BLMM/M4BL-affiliated organizations was that of Rekia Boyd, an unarmed twenty-two-year-old Black woman killed by off-duty detective Dante Servin in 2012 in the North Lawndale community of Chicago. When news of the killing broke, veteran organizer Crista Noel of the Women's All Points Bulletin, who was also a member of the Chicago Alliance against Racist and Political Repression, immediately reached out to Boyd's family. She worked with them to pressure the state's attorney Anita Alvarez to indict Servin.[11] Mariame

Kaba was another person who got involved in the case early on, speaking on panels organized by Crista and mobilizing others.

Servin's defense was that he supposedly thought one of Boyd's friends had a gun, so he opened fire in fear for his life. The friend, whom Servin shot in the hand, was actually holding a cell phone. Boyd's family was awarded $4.5 million in a wrongful death suit against the city—years before Servin was tried. Eventually, nearly two years after Boyd's death, and after considerable protest and agitation, Servin was charged with involuntary manslaughter, making him the first Chicago police officer in more than fifteen years to face criminal charges in a fatal shooting. A judge ultimately acquitted Servin in a 2015 trial.[12]

After the acquittal of Dante Servin, Rekia's case was taken up by BYP100, A Long Walk Home, Black youth activists like Veronica Morris-Moore (of Fearless Leading by the Youth), and others. Rather than dampening their spirits, Servin's acquittal galvanized Chicago activists and organizers, who rallied behind the demand to "fire Dante Servin." #FireDanteServin was an abolitionist campaign whose demands looked beyond the prison system for some measure of justice.[13] Boyd's brother, Martinez Sutton, and her mother were vigilant in keeping the memory of their family member alive. Over the past few years, BLM Chicago, BYP100, Assata's Daughters, the Women's All Points Bulletin, the Chicago Alliance against Racist and Political Repression, We Charge Genocide, and the Let Us Breathe Collective have all organized vigils, protests, and disruptions of Chicago Police Board meetings, demanding accountability in Boyd's case and showing up in a sea of bright yellow T-shirts emblazoned with "Fire Dante Servin" on them. To preempt his likely firing, Servin resigned from the Chicago Police Department in May 2016 and was thus able to keep his lucrative pension.[14] The campaign was nonetheless a powerful show of force and unity by Chicago's anti–police violence movement.

The tactics throughout the #FireDanteServin and #RememberRekia campaign were bold and unrelenting. At more than one meeting of the Chicago Police Board, widely criticized for its pro-police bias and ineffectiveness, BYP100 literally shut the meeting down to expose the board as a public relations unit for the mayor. At one particularly heated board meeting, the barely five-foot-tall organizer Charlene Carruthers shouted down the board members, insisting they acknowledge that they had not indicted a single officer in the many cases that had come before them and were in essence a farce.[15] In the same vein, BYP100 organizer Rachel Williams gave a tough and eloquent speech addressing the body as the "unelected board," and activist Damon Williams confronted the group as "illegitimate," putting them in the spotlight and on the defensive. These actions eventually forced the City of Chicago to rethink and revise its mechanisms of political accountability altogether. Throughout the "Justice for Rekia" campaign, the overwhelmingly Black Chicago State University was on the verge of closure, owing to lack of state funds. Activists linked that economic and education justice issue to the issue of police violence. In the words of BYP100 organizer Joan Fadayiro, "We see these struggles as intrinsically connected. The City of Chicago and the State of Illinois are proving that they do not value black lives. Police officers are enabled to kill black women with impunity while black community assets such as Chicago State University are divested from."[16]

The spring 2015 formation of Assata's Daughters, to cultivate the leadership of Black women and girls and uphold the legacy of radical women activists like Assata Shakur, was a significant development in Chicago's political ecosystem. Page May, a Black Vermont native with a sharp tongue, a quick wit, and a fearless persona, spearheaded the group's founding. The members immediately joined in the city's ongoing protests, and were catalysts for others.

Assata's Daughters was part of a coalition called The Collective, which also included Fearless Leading by the Youth, Black Lives Matter Chicago (BLM-CHI), and others. The group combined brazen direct-action tactics with a bit of political theater when, on April 30, 2016, they shut down Lakeshore Drive, one of Chicago's main traffic arteries, to disrupt the NFL draft, which the city was proudly hosting. Borrowing from and reinterpreting imagery from Beyoncé's Super Bowl "Black Power" performance and *Lemonade* video and album, protesters wore black outfits with red berets and chained themselves together with fists clenched in the air. They insisted they were protesting the lack of funding for public education and the refusal of the mayor to fire the police officer who gunned down unarmed Rekia Boyd. After a prolonged standoff, police cut the chains that bound the protesters together and arrested seventeen people.[17]

Anchoring the work of BLM-CHI since 2015 is a tight-knit core of organizers led by savvy activist Aislinn Pulley. Aislinn, who grew up in an activist family, moves and speaks slowly and methodically. She is never flippant. She brings this same care and attention to detail to BLM-CHI, which has spent a great deal of time reaching out to and cultivating relationships with the families of victims of police violence, and has also supported fundraising efforts to aid victims of intracommunal violence as well. Those families are almost always in need of emotional and financial support. BLM-CHI has made a point of raising burial funds for victims of police violence. The names are not abstract. Aislinn and her comrades have been committed to personalizing the stories of individual victims and their extended families.

In their speeches and literature, they have also connected state violence and intracommunal (street) violence, pointing out that the lack of housing, jobs, and education are the factors fueling Chicago's street-level gun violence.

From the struggle for education justice to the #RememberRekia campaign, women activists in Chicago, including queer women, have been central, visible, and vocal since 2013—so much so that a prominent local news magazine, the *Chicago Reader,* published a feature aptly entitled "Queer Women Are Shaping Chicago's Black Lives Matter Movement." In the words of Rachel Williams, as quoted in the article, "Let's be real: Most of the work is being led by Black queer women. We're not going to be put in a box or left out."[18]

Still in her twenties in 2015, Veronica Morris-Moore is another Black queer activist who has been an important leader in Chicago politics. Although many groups and individuals were involved, Veronica was instrumental in the large, layered, and protracted campaign to force the University of Chicago, one of the most powerful and well-endowed universities in the country, to establish an adult trauma center on the South Side of the city. The backstory of the campaign is important, and the outcome was almost unprecedented. In 2010 a young activist, Damien Turner, then eighteen years old, was the victim of a random drive-by shooting in a neighborhood rife with gun violence. The ambulance had to drive him ten miles to reach the closest trauma center. He died. Turner was an organizer with a South Side group, STOP (Southsider Together Organizing for Power), and one of the cofounders of FLY (Fearless Leading by the Youth). His death hit the young Black activist community hard. Its members launched a five-year campaign that included direct-action tactics, the disruption of an alumni gala, and bold tactics to shame the university into creating a forty-million-dollar trauma center that will go a long way toward saving Black lives. Many victims of gun violence in Chicago are within a short drive of the University of Chicago. Morris-Moore drew large conclusions from a weighty local victory, concluding, "Liberation is completely possible when people come together and organize."[19] The trauma center victory was not tantamount to liberation, but the gist of Morris-Moore's point was right, and others took it to heart. No progress would be made without determined and relentless organizing, and with that the seemingly unattainable was within reach.

The local work in Chicago has been important on its own terms; however, a number of Chicago activists have had an impact far beyond the city itself. Some are well-known, while others are not. Dara Cooper's name may not be well-known beyond movement circles, but she has been a consistent and influential force within it. As an informal advisor to the emergent M4BL and a member of the policy table that drafted the "Vision for Black Lives" document, Dara has worked on food justice, educating many of us about the importance of our ability, or inability, to feed ourselves, and about our connection to land and food. She has made her home in Chicago; Jackson, Mississippi; Atlanta; and Philadelphia over the past decade. Dara's work with the National Black Food Justice Alliance and her research and activism on food hubs, food cooperatives, and the larger issue of food sovereignty have made sure that BLMM/M4BL activists are sensitized to these issues. All of this began in Chicago, where Dara was working to combat so-called food deserts, mostly in Black and Brown communities, through the innovative concept of a healthy-food bus that was a kind of mobile farmers' market providing healthy produce in communities where it was otherwise unavailable. In Dara's view, the absence of food sovereignty is a special kind of violence.

Chicago organizers have engaged in numerous protests over the years, but in November 2015, when the bone-chilling video of unarmed Black teenager Laquan McDonald being shot sixteen times by Chicago police officer Jason Van Dyke was released, protests began anew. This time they targeted the mayor, the police chief, and the state's attorney. Significantly, some of the BLMM/M4BL organizers were not explicitly calling for Van Dyke to be jailed—since many of them were prison abolitionists. More important, they called for his firing as they worked to expose the larger issue of institutional racism that often leads to such wrongdoing: the code of silence that allows for cover-ups; the city officials who suppressed details of McDonald's killing; and the state's attorney, who, they argued, was more interested in maintaining good relations with the police department than in realizing justice for a Black teen from a poor neighborhood.

The Laquan McDonald video was conveniently kept away from the public until after Chicago's heated mayoral election and was released only after journalists like Brandon Smith filed a lawsuit to get the tape released, and Jamie Kalven of the Invisible Institute, acting on a tip, did some "guerilla research" and exposed the existence of the tape and the cover-up that followed.[20] Another systemic problem that activists addressed was the ways in which police unions have negotiated labor contracts that protect police from full disclosure and swift accountability for misdeeds. After thousands of people took to the streets in protest, Van Dyke was eventually arrested and charged with first-degree murder. It was the first time in thirty-five years that a Chicago police officer had been charged with murder while on duty.[21] Dante Servin's shooting of Rekia Boyd was an off-duty incident.

The McDonald murder garnered national and international media attention, and many Chicago activist groups were propelled into action around the case. The chant "Sixteen shots and a cover-up" reverberated throughout the city as the mantra of a campaign that included groups that existed long before the emergence of BLMM/M4BL. Among them were Action Now, STOP, SOUL (Southsiders Organizing for Unity and Liberation), the Workers Center for Racial Justice, and the Reverend Jesse Jackson's Rainbow PUSH Coalition, all filling the streets in sometimes uneasy alliance. One night a series of street protests shut down the South Loop area west of downtown; scuffles broke out with police, and there were several arrests. The street protests and disruptions of city meetings and mayoral speeches, as well as negative attention from local, national, and alternative media, continued, eventually forcing the city to do something. Mayor Rahm Emanuel fired the chief of police, Garry McCarthy, in December 2015 and, in a tearful press conference, apologized to city residents for not handling the Laquan McDonald case better. The timing was all too convenient. Emanuel had just survived an unprecedented run-off election against progressive Latinx challenger Jesus (Chuy) Garcia. Had the video been released before the election, the outcome might have been different.

After McCarthy's departure, there was still the unapologetic state's attorney, Anita Alvarez, a conservative Latinx Democrat, who had been consistently insensitive and even hostile to community concerns. She was up for reelection three months after the video's release and had been implicated in its suppression. Local groups, including BLMM/M4BL activists, launched one of the most creative electoral campaigns the city had seen: the #ByeAnita campaign. They followed Alvarez to fundraisers and demanded answers. They held vigils outside her offices. They even rented a propeller plane to fly over the city with a banner that read, "ByeAnita." They unfurled large banners, handed out flyers all over the city (while chanting "Sixteen shots and a cover-up"), and created a firestorm on social media. They were creative and unrelenting in their campaign to expose her record and urge voters to oust her from office. One of the most active groups in this campaign was Assata's Daughters.

The #ByeAnita campaign refrained from endorsing an opposition candidate but focused rather on the platform "Anita must go." She suffered a rousing defeat to progressive African American attorney Kim Foxx in the Democratic primary, with a significant uptick in the number of young people who went to the polls. Foxx went on to win the March 2016 election.[22]

It is important to note that the work of BLMM/M4BL and other newer formations built upon preexisting organizing efforts, such as that of the Chicago Alliance against Racist and Political Repression, a multiracial leftist group that emerged in the early 1970s out of the campaign to free Angela Davis and currently leads campaigns against police violence and abuse. The alliance was the catalyst for the ongoing demand for a Civilian Police Accountability Council in Chicago, which has growing support. With seventy-plus-year-old veteran activist Frank Chapman, a large man with a baritone voice, a humble manner, and a lot of political savvy, at the helm, it has been a critical part of the Black Freedom Movement in Chicago.

One outcome of these important efforts has been the strengthened relationships between different sectors of Chicago's activist community, including its Black and Latinx sectors. Notably, new ties were forged between Mijente, a national left-leaning Latinx group[23] and a leading force in the immigrant rights movement, and BYP100. Organized Communities against Deportations, led by an amazing activist family, the Carasco-Unzuetas, is a local affiliate of Mijente. Mijente and BYP100 are wrestling with ways of building a movement against the criminalization of immigrant and Black working-class communities through the notion of "expanded sanctuary." This work highlights the violent, coercive, and carceral solutions for a wide range of social and economic issues impacting poor communities of color in the United States—citizens, legal immigrants, and the undocumented. As Marisa Franco of Mijente points out, "There is no time for our ideas of sanctuaries to be exclusive. Sanctuaries must include not only undocumented people, but also non-immigrant Muslims, LGBTQIA people, Black and Indigenous folks and political dissidents."[24] In Chicago, the Expanded Sanctuary campaign has called for an end to the discriminatory "gang database," as well as to immigration raids and deportations. The Expanded Sanctuary campaign experienced a small but significant victory in January 2018. After waging a campaign against his unfair incarceration by Immigration and Customs Enforcement, Organized Communities against Deportations and its allies won the release of Wilmer Catalan-Ramirez, a young undocumented father, who had been unfairly detained because he was incorrectly listed in the city's gang database.

Another group that has been a catalyst for building bridges between different organizing hubs is the Let Us Breathe Collective in Chicago, founded after brother and sister artists Kristiana Rae Colón and Damon Williams visited Ferguson during the uprising. They returned to Chicago; helped with a film about the Lost Voices group, which they befriended while they were in Ferguson; and then began to build the Let Us Breathe social justice arts collective, centered around Black and Latinx artist-activists. Damon had also been involved with BYP100.

The Let Us Breathe Collective's biggest action was a forty-one-day encampment called Freedom Square that took place in summer 2016. The encampment, in Chicago's North Lawndale neighborhood, was pitched on a vacant lot right across from the notorious Homan Square, a Chicago Police Department "black site" that was exposed by the *Guardian* newspaper as a place where African American arrestees were taken and were reportedly roughed up and sometimes tortured without any official record and without ever being charged. Freedom Square also became a space for experimenting with collective decision making, self-governance, dispute resolution, building a sharing economy, and incorporating art into protest. Dozens of activists and artists camped out in tents and built a makeshift kitchen, library, and free store. Many hard lessons were learned there too. For example, many of the complicated and intractable problems faced by poor Black communities in Chicago landed in that dusty little square—interpersonal violence, substance abuse, and other traumas that the committed core of artists simply did not have the capacity to fully meet. Freedom Square was still an inspiration to many. The encampment raised visibility of the nefarious practices of the police and provided a gathering space for Chicago activists to converge, to talk, to collaborate, and to serve the community by volunteering in a number of capacities. When the open-air encampment ended, Damon, Kristiana, and Let Us Breathe members Jennifer Pagan, Bella Bhah, Cherisse Jackson, and others helped to found the Breathing Room, an indoor social justice art space that welcomes and partners with an array of the city's radical and progressive groups to host events and meetings and provide limited services and support. For a time, the Breathing Room was also home to BLM-CHI; Ujimma Medics, a group that trains community members to treat gunshot victims; and Brave Space Alliance, a group of transgender activists led by LaSaia Wade, a dynamic indigenous Afro–Puerto Rican trans woman.

Between 2012 and 2017, Chicago witnessed a steady growth in collaboration between different progressive organizations that are intergenerational and transcend racial and ethnic neighborhoods and boundaries. Campaigns, in addition to the campaigns already cited, included the 2012 Chicago Teachers' Union strike, which garnered widespread community support; the Fight for 15 Chicago campaigns; and the Dyett High School hunger strike to defend public neighborhood schools, led by education activist Jitu Brown, members of the Kenwood Oakland Community Organization, and Teachers for Social Justice.

Finally, there is the "Resist. Reimagine. Rebuild." coalition, which I work closely with. Formed after the 2016 November presidential election and involving over thirty grassroots and labor organizations, it is affiliated with M4BL's newly formed people of color–led multiracial coalition The Majority, which promises to "build an anti-racist Left for radical democracy." "Resist. Reimagine. Rebuild." led a major, primarily people of color contingent in the city's 2017 May Day march and has organized numerous teach-ins and community forums. The 2019 mayoral race will certainly be another pivotal moment for Chicago's new and old coalitions. BLMM/M4BL organizers continue to be at the center of the work.

EIGHT

Political Quilters and Maroon Spaces

In the early 2000s, I was a part of a national collective that we called Ella's Daughters. Inspired by the tradition of Ella Baker, we engaged in what we called political quilting, working to build bridges and responsiveness among different sectors of the national progressive community of scholars, activists, and artists. I later learned that the Center for Third World Organizing in Oakland used a similar movement-building metaphor— "weaving cloth." The idea here is that, in order to sustain a powerful mass movement, we need to forge strong and reinforcing ties between our various communities, organizations, and movement sectors as we work to connect all the strands, to stitch—or weave together—disparate patches of struggle.

Building connections between distinct organizing communities is one important task of movement-building, and creating arenas in which trust and collaboration can be forged and collective thinking can occur is another. Modern maroon spaces, in a sense, are ones where organizers can come together, fortify themselves to face the brutal terrain of everyday struggle, and forge new levels of consensus. It is important to note that maroonage, in the era of slavery, was not simply about escape. Maroon communities—communities of fugitive slaves and their descendants—built semiautonomous spaces, but they also often confronted and fought against slave empires. Since 2014, three entities have served as maroon spaces, providing refuge and connectivity, retreat spaces, and training grounds for movement organizations and individuals. They are Black Organizing for Leadership and Dignity (BOLD), Blackbird, and the BlackOUT Collective (BOC).

BOLD has been an incubator for organizers who have taken their place at the forefront of BLMM/M4BL. Founded in 2012, BOLD has trained more than three hundred activists working in critical movement organizations throughout the country. The three pillars of BOLD's training are political education, transformational organizing, and embodied leadership (relying on theories of somatic therapy). Denise Perry, a fifty-something Black, queer feminist and former labor organizer based in Miami, who is the principal force behind BOLD, is revered within movement circles for her quiet strength and clarity. The group conducts a series of week-long intensive workshops and trainings several times a year for cohorts of Black nonprofit workers and administrators. Its main training site is a reclaimed slave plantation in North Carolina. Alicia Garza and Opal Tometi met each other at a BOLD training session.

BOLD's mission is to train and sustain a generation of capable and healthy Black leaders, who can support one another and the growing movement. But the ever-humble Perry, who has been referred to lovingly as the Harriet Tubman of the movement (leading BOLD participants to freedom over treacherous terrain), will quickly add, "BOLD is family." She signs her email notes, "Black Love." In this way she and her comrade, organizer, trainer, and movement intellectual Sendolo Diaminah (BOLD's program coordinator) aim not only to impart tangible skills to Black organizers but also to aid them in creating community and a support network that can help to sustain activists for the long haul. BOLD's explicit mission is "to facilitate social transformation and fundamental improvements in the lives and living conditions of Black people by (re)building the social justice infrastructure required to organize Black communities."[1]

While the names of a number of BOLD alumni are recognizable in media accounts of BLMM/M4BL actions, many of those in the BOLD family were doing slow and steady organizing well before August 9, 2014, and have continued to do so since then, plugging away and supporting major mobilizations as they arise. BOLD trainings and retreats have created interstitial spaces of reflection, community building, and skill acquisition that occur during low points in public mass-movement action or serve as temporary oases for reflection when things become especially intense. BOLD is a space where Black organizers dedicated to long-term social justice come together to connect and retool. And when new opportunities arise, or crises develop, they often organize with one another, independent of BOLD. Political quilters like the leaders of BOLD create opportunities for making critical connections. In Perry's words, BOLD is "working to unleash Black-led organizing, placing the power to transform and govern this country in the hands of its most marginalized communities."[2]

Another, newer set of political quilters is made up of the three founders of Blackbird—Thenjiwe McHarris, Mervyn Marcano, and Maurice (Moe) Mitchell. Originally a group of Brooklyn-based resource mobilizers, conveners, and consensus and capacity builders, they have had a large influence on the evolution of the movement since Ferguson. The Blackbird founders had known one another through their participation in the Malcolm X Grassroots Movement years earlier but had not worked closely together as a team. They reconnected in Ferguson and decided to pool their energies and mobilize their skills in service to the growing movement. All were profoundly moved by the courage and resolve of the Ferguson protesters, and all decided to quit their jobs in 2014 to devote themselves full-time to movement-building work. "We chose to lean into risk" in making a commitment to the struggle that had been ignited in Ferguson, McHarris recalled. Mitchell took a leave from his job to embed himself in the Ferguson struggle from August through December 2014.³ He walked the streets of Ferguson, facilitated meetings and strategy sessions, reached out to networks of activists and allies throughout the country, and listened to the ideas and frustrations of the new activists he met there.

McHarris brought an important perspective and skill set with her to Ferguson as well. Having grown up in a working-class Black family in the Bronx in the 1980s and '90s, McHarris had been exposed to political organizing and theory through her membership in the Malcolm X Grassroots Movement for several years. Then, as a staff person for several NGOs, and a participant in a number of UN forums, she had traveled throughout the world, notably throughout the African Diaspora, and witnessed anticolonial and postcolonial struggles firsthand from South Africa to Brazil. She read the global implications of what was happening in Ferguson in the summer and fall of 2014.

Ferguson was as much a baptism by fire for the Blackbird founders and other national activists who migrated there as it was for locals. In McHarris's words, "The momentum of the moment propelled things forward. It [Ferguson] was a political laboratory that allowed people to engage in ways they had not done before."

Despite the intensity of the situation on the ground, the events were not as random as some media depictions have suggested. "There was a certain rigor" to the discussions that were going on, McHarris recalls, marked by daily planning sessions leading up to Ferguson October, the massive protests planned and timed to coincide with the grand jury's expected decision about whether to indict Darren Wilson. McHarris recounts that she and her Blackbird comrades urged local leaders to "nationalize" the struggle, knowing that if other activists came from around the country, they would be catalyzed and inspired.[4] The groups and individuals who had invested in Ferguson began planning a "Shut It Down" campaign once the nonindictment verdict was announced. While the team that would soon form Blackbird embraced the mantra "High impact, low ego" and kept under the radar of many outside observers, their role by all accounts was critical. "We had a theory of change," Mitchell observed, "that sought to build local and national capacity simultaneously."[5]

After Ferguson October, in which tens of thousands of people protested, marched, and rallied, activists gathered in New York in December 2014 for a strategy meeting at which the Movement for Black Lives coalition was formed. After that was a Los Angeles meeting, and finally a core of activists converged on Selma, Alabama, in March 2015 for the fiftieth anniversary of the historic 1965 civil rights march across the Edmund Pettus Bridge, known as Bloody Sunday because of the terror that local sheriffs unleashed on peaceful Black protesters. There the activists took the opportunity, with history as their backdrop, to meet and hone plans for the new M4BL formation.

One of Blackbird's signature contributions to the movement was its role in helping to organize the major July 2015 convening on the campus of Cleveland State University, which brought over two thousand Black organizers together under the M4BL banner. Thereafter, the M4BL coalition organized seven national "tables," or committees intended to combine and coordinate forces. Those tables—strategy, action, communications, policy, organizing, electoral strategy, and resources—have representatives from BYP100, Dream Defenders, Black Lives Matter Global Network, Southerners on New Ground, Organization for Black Struggle, and dozens of other national and local organizations. In fall 2017, M4BL launched its Electoral Justice Project, headed up by political strategist Jessica Byrd and St. Louis activist Kayla Reed, as well as Mississippi-based lawyer and activist Rukia Lumumba, with the intent of supporting electoral engagement on its own terms in order to contend for power through a strong, independent, and radical Black infrastructure.

Since 2014, Blackbird has secured funding and grown its staff to include a cohort of talented young organizers and strategists: Karl Kumodzi, Marbre Stahly-Butts, and Iman Young. Key individuals (not already mentioned) who have provided political and intellectual leadership to the M4BL tables coordinated by Blackbird staff include M. Adams, a Madison, Wisconsin–based activist and the leader of Freedom Inc., an organization that works with low- and no-income people of color communities; and Ash-Lee Henderson, who refers to herself as an "Afrilachian," a Black Appalachian from Tennessee. In 2017, Henderson was in her early thirties but already had over a decade of organizing experience under her belt, having worked with Project South, Students against Sweatshops, and other organizing efforts. And finally there is Cazembe Jackson, a trans man based in Atlanta, who was for a time a national organizer for Freedom Road Socialist Organization. These three, among many others, have influenced the politics and direction of the group.

Anchored by the Blackbird staff, and reflecting the strength and lucidity of its constituent groups, the "Vision for Black Lives" policy platform produced in August 2016 is the second significant accomplishment of the M4BL effort. Stahly-Butts, a lawyer who worked for years combating racism in the criminal justice system, played a leadership role in its coordination. The "Vision for Black Lives," which took over a year to complete and included input from dozens of progressive Black-led organizations and individual scholars and researchers, tackled a broad set of issues, from cash bonds to climate change, to Palestine. A set of actions and policy remedies was proposed for each problem. Writing in the *Boston Review,* Robin D. G. Kelley adeptly summarized the importance of the comprehensive document as follows: it is "a plan for ending structural racism, saving the planet, and transforming the entire nation—not just Black lives."[6] If not for the racism and shortsightedness that still plague certain sectors of the predominantly white Left, the "Vision for Black Lives" would have been embraced as a movement manifesto that, while rooted in Black struggles, speaks to a thoroughly broad-based set of progressive issues.

Finally, the third group of "political quilters" is the Black woman–led BOC, also formed during Ferguson October, which organizes direct-action training for local and national organizations. One media review described them as "the badass women" who "shut shit down." The term *shut shit down,* ubiquitous in M4BL circles, signals a rejection of the politics of respectability and the notion that actions deemed undignified or impolite are off limits. In choosing to shut shit down, activists are calling for change and attention through disruption and are forcefully insisting that people not "dance on the bodies of the dead," as one poetic protestor put it. The BOC was cofounded by two women with long histories of organizing, despite their relatively young ages: Chinyere

Tutashinda and Celeste Faison. They are also active in the M4BL coalition, along with their fellow BlackOUT trainer Karissa Lewis, an urban farmer and activist, who also serves as the executive director of Oakland's Center for Third World Organizing. In reflecting on BlackOUT's approach to training and tactical support, Chinyere indicated, "Direct action as a tactic is one that black people have been using for hundreds of years, from worker slow-downs to sit-ins. We see our work as connecting to that tradition."[7]

From their base in Oakland, BOC members travel around the country doing direct-action and preparedness training. They have helped local organizers shut down bridges, highways, buildings, and meetings. Celeste Faison, who now works for the National Domestic Workers Alliance, took a short leave from her job as a youth organizer to join the 2014 protests in Ferguson and was moved by the courage and determination she witnessed there. At one point Faison observed protesters late at night literally walking up and down the street and looping back to do the same thing over and over again. She thought to herself that she and others were in positions to offer more creative tactics to the work. The group that would later form the BOC began to brainstorm ways to do just that. They eventually developed workshops to teach organizers techniques to make direct actions more effective, dynamic, and impactful.

Black Brunch came out of the efforts of the BOC and other Oakland-area activists in December 2014 and January 2015. For this quietly disruptive strategy, groups of protesters went into ritzy restaurants during Sunday brunch in cities like Oakland and New York to read the names of Black victims of police violence to mimosa-drinking patrons, before being forced by management to leave.

The BOC's actions are also similar to but bolder than the civil rights–era Student Nonviolent Coordinating Committee's civil disobedience trainings. Its behind-the-scenes movement-builders have been invaluable resources for the growing force of BLMM/M4BL. The BOC has been a leading force in the BLMM/M4BL policy, strategy, and action tables.

BOLD, Blackbird, and the BOC play solidifying and cohering roles in the BLMM/M4BL ecosystem. While none are base-building or mass organizations, they all provide the support, resources, and connective tissue needed to bind together different pieces of the whole, and bolster individual organizations and the movement overall.

Conclusion

No one is free until we all are free [to paraphrase
Fannie Lou Hamer], and that includes those who are
employed, unemployed, those who are incarcerated
or in gangs, or who are sex workers. What we are
fighting for is a world where our full humanity is
honored and protected and valued, and that includes
all of who we are.

Aislinn Pulley

Ruth Wilson Gilmore is a radical intellectual and one of the
most prominent advocates for prison abolition in the country.
Her advocacy is anything but simple. To move toward the abolition of prisons (the inhumane practice of caging human beings),
she argues, is to get involved with an intensive process of building: jobs, housing, new cultural practices, and new ways of
thinking about work, rights, restorative justice, and community.
Ruth Gilmore and her collaborator and partner, Craig Gilmore,
point out that control of Black bodies, poor bodies, resistant
bodies, and labor in general "first required extralegal violence,
but later the legitimacy of the badge replaced the discredited
Klan hood."[1] Here is what they have to say about the Black Lives
Matter Movement/Movement for Black Lives (BLMM/M4BL):

"Sparked by police murder in capitalism's neoliberal turn, the post-Ferguson movement may therefore be understood as protests against profound austerity and the iron fist necessary to impose it. The movement's central challenge is to prevent the work from facilitating another transition in regimes of policing and incarceration, displacement and disinvestment through formal but not transformative reforms."[2]

Gilmore's challenge to BLMM/M4BL is this: the movement must resist any push to narrow and constrain its goals or to decontextualize them from the larger political landscape of racial capitalism. Gilmore's analysis also poses a challenge to the predominately white Left: Is the Left willing to repudiate the "class only" postracialism that some white and a few Black intellectuals have argued for? That line of thinking wrongly suggests that those organizing around the special oppression of women, LGBTQIA folks, Blacks, Latinx, and indigenous peoples have contributed to a fragmentation of the Left and divided the working class. The truth is that the Left and the working class were never monolithic or unified. Exploitation has always been experienced unevenly, to say the least. And racism, sexism, homophobia, and chauvinisms of various sorts have done more to divide and weaken the Left than those organizing to combat these injustices. Moreover, an *intersectional analysis*—a term that was coined by legal scholar and activist Kimberlé Crenshaw but has been advocated by Black feminists from Audre Lorde and Barbara Smith to the Combahee River Collective, bell hooks, Angela Davis, and others—sees the class struggle as intimately bound up with the struggle against all the other major forms of oppression. There is a symbiosis between US and European capitalism, empire, white supremacy, and hetero-patriarchy. This understanding is a basis for unity, not fragmentation. If only the various white-led Left and labor organizations could truly internalize these historical truths, the political possibilities would be enormous.

Gilmore also echoes the call by sociologist André Gorz for campaigns targeting "non-reformist reforms"—those demands that plant the seeds for systemic change and challenge the very logic of the profit system.[3] This is what Gilmore and her abolitionist comrades are arguing for, and their ideas are gaining traction.

Framing the BLMM/M4BL campaigns in global and historical context is another critical ingredient for transformative change. Indicting the economic underpinnings of police control and violence is another. And forging a practice that not only includes but also centers the interests of the most oppressed and marginalized sectors of the Black community is also key. Finally, looking to a Black-led multiracial mass movement is inescapable, as Keeanga-Yamahtta Taylor insists in her book *From #BlackLivesMatter to Black Liberation.* Embracing a long-term vision, Taylor writes, "The challenge before us is to connect the current struggle to end police terror in our communities with an even larger movement to transform this country in such a way that the police are no longer needed to respond to the consequences of that inequality."[4]

As I have argued in *Dissent* and elsewhere, BLMM/M4BL can be viewed as a Black-led class struggle—informed by, grounded in, and bolstered by Black feminist politics. This is evidenced by its links to the low-wage worker movement, through Alicia Garza's leadership role in the National Domestic Workers Alliance, BYP100's collaborative efforts with the Fight for 15 and its "Agenda to Build Black Futures" economic justice campaign, and Dream Defenders' opposition to capitalism. Over and over, BLMM/M4BL leaders and organizers have insisted not only that racial justice must include economic justice and vice versa but that the two are intimately connected. Writing in *Jacobin,* Shawn Gude makes the point powerfully: "Baltimore, then, is like so many other cities with their own Freddie Grays: a place in which private capital has left enormous sections of the city to rot, where a chasm separates the life chances of black and white residents—and where cops *brutally patrol* a population deemed *disposable*."[5] Gwen Carr, the mother of Eric Garner, the African American father of four who was killed by police on Staten Island while trying to break up a fight but who was known to local cops for the minor "crime" of selling loosies (single unpackaged cigarettes), put it this way:

> My son Eric died last year at the hands of the men who were supposed to protect him. At the time he was selling cigarettes to support his family. These two things are, of course, connected. They reflect the ongoing struggle the black community faces every day for racial and economic justice. They're at the heart of the Black Lives Matter movement. Eric's senseless death has forced our country to confront the toxic effects of police brutality. My hope is that together, we can also change the system that trapped him and so many black men and women across our city and nation in poverty, too.[6]

A core of BLMM/M4BL leaders have taken Gwen Carr's words to heart, forging a praxis that centers class, gender, sexuality, and empire alongside race to reflect a truly intersectional analysis.

Why is this analysis important? It represents a set of politics and practices that hold up and enact the radical spirit of the 1977 Combahee River Collective statement. The Combahee collective was a Boston-based activist group of Black lesbian feminists, who were also unapologetically socialist. They wrote, "We realize that the liberation of all oppressed peoples necessitates the destruction of the political-economic systems of capitalism and imperialism as well as patriarchy. We are socialists because we believe that work must be organized for the collective benefit of those who do the work and create the products, and not for the profit of the bosses. Material resources must be equally distributed among those who create these resources. We are not convinced, however, that a socialist revolution that is not also a feminist and anti-racist revolution will guarantee our liberation."[7] The group would come to included the late Black feminist icon Audre Lorde; New Jersey–based scholar-activist Cheryl Clarke; Demita Frazier; Kitchen Table Press publisher Barbara Smith and her sister, Beverly Smith; scholar-activist Margo Okazama Ray; and the current "first lady" of New York City, Chirlane McCray, who has traveled a long, interesting, and circuitous path since 1977.[8] Over time, many Black radical thinkers like the Combahee founders have come to view that revolution as a process rather than an event.

Contrary to the shortsighted argument that groups like the Combahee River Collective and its offshoots are the epitome of "divisive identity politics," Combahee River's expansive and inclusive radical statement proves exactly the opposite. It begins by locating its authors in the hierarchy of the society and world we live in and grounds them in a set of lived experiences that create the basis for (but are not *determinative* of) their radical critique of the status quo—capitalism, empire, white supremacy, and hetero-patriarchy. The year 2017 marked the fortieth anniversary of the Combahee River Collective statement, and panels, conferences, articles, and strategy sessions have revisited the document, reclaimed it, and affirmed its continued relevance. The National Women's Studies Association was proud to host its 2017 national conference in Baltimore, entitled "Combahee at 40: Feminist Scholars and Activists Engage the Movement for Black Lives," which did just that.

Still, there remains work to be done—contradictions to sort out, debates to be had, stories to share, strategies to sharpen, and even some wounds to heal. Activists should not underestimate the profound seriousness of this work.

And so, what is needed? More organizations with "on-ramps" and portals of entry, so those who are now spectators can move toward action and find a way into the work. More national campaigns that bring activists from various sectors together with focused strategic purpose. We can think of the ongoing national coalition-building and united-front work as a wheel with spokes rather than a hierarchical, top-down pyramid. But the wheel has to have a hub and a center to connect the spokes (i.e., local and issue-specific struggles). And there needs to be more serious and rigorous political education, in terms of both history and theory.

To say this country is in a difficult political moment is an understatement, as neo-Nazis march across the South brandishing torches, as they did in Charlottesville, Virginia, in the summer of 2017. The reckless and racist policies of the Trump presidential administration have put many vulnerable populations in peril and on the defensive. The Department of Justice is moving away from even giving lip service to police reform or accountability, and is advancing policies to increase the number of prisons and extend the reach of surveillance and the punishment industry. Social programs, health care, and public services will be deeply impacted by the horrendous 2017 tax bill, which promises to be what economist Jeffrey Sachs has bluntly described as the biggest public "heist" ever—stealing resources from the poor to fatten the bank accounts of the wealthy.[9] The third version of the so-called Muslim ban has gone into effect, making it difficult, and in some cases impossible, for those from predominantly Muslim countries to even visit the United States. The anti-immigrant rhetoric of the Trump administration threatens more deportations and harassment of undocumented residents. The threat of repression remains real as Trump praises and cavorts with dictators around the world, and maligns the media at home. The attack on net neutrality (through attempts to privatize and further commodify the Internet and social media) means organizers risk losing a powerful tool for organizing and communicating. And moves toward deregulation mean corporations can take calculated risks at public expense, with little recourse for citizens.

Still, I am reminded of a quote from philosopher Homi Bhabha, brought to my attention by my colleague Roderick Ferguson, that references a longer quote from Walter Benjamin: "the state of emergency is also always a state of emergence."[10] Already there has been an upsurge and intensification in organizing, coalition building, united-front formations, and serious strategizing in the Left, including the Black Left. Bernie Sanders's 2016 presidential campaign, as lacking as it was on the issues of race and white supremacy, nevertheless widened the debate about the failings of capitalism and the possibility for alternatives. The growth of left-leaning groups like Democratic Socialists of America, Our Revolution, Indivisible, and the Working Families Party has the potential to pull US politics to the left, if and only if they take seriously the scourge of white supremacy and the generative and transformative power of the Black insurgent impulse. The Majority coalition, promising to "build an anti-racist Left for radical democracy," and the newly formed LeftRoots, a people of color–led socialist organization heavily influenced by the lessons from the left movements in Latin America, are already organizing with that understanding in place. All of this is to ask the question—what comes next? We look to the new generation of organizers, dreamers, visionaries, and freedom fighters to forge out of this current state of emergency, this current bleak moment, a new path, for Black people, for all people, and for the planet.

Epilogue

A Personal Reflection

I struggled to complete this book while engaging in and supporting the ongoing resistance against a new protofascist turn in US politics, one in which racism, misogyny, and all varieties of xenophobia are alarmingly pronounced. In my effort to make sense of an ever-changing national and global landscape, I hope this book makes some small contribution to the freedom-making work that lies ahead of us. If Alicia Garza's initial Facebook post in 2013 was a love letter to Black people, this epilogue is a love letter to the organizers in the Movement for Black Lives, and a tribute to their increasingly expansive vision.

First of all, thank you. Thank you for your courage and your passion, for your savvy and your boldness. Thank you for facing the bloody reality—embedded in the historical fibers of this country and become all too routine—and saying "no." And in saying no you brazenly rejected the bourgeois trappings of respectability. In other words, you said "hell, no" to state violence in its crudest form, as well as to the slow death that racial capitalism and its neoliberal practices have caused over time.

Your practice reflects an understanding that only when elites
cannot buy you off, dazzle you with their power, intoxicate you with
a sense of your own importance, and tempt you with trinkets and
access and money and celebrity can you be truly engaged in a liberatory process of freedom making. For many of you, this time has
come. When amazing Chicago organizer Aislinn Pulley declined an
invitation to the White House without blinking, because she did not
want to be a part of a photo op with no outcome, we all felt a little
freer. When Black Brunch protesters strolled into fancy eateries and
began "impolitely" talking about Black death, breaking the bubble of
denial that shrouds yuppie privilege, we knew we were a little bit
freer. When you refused to be Al Sharpton's protégés or political
accessories, or the human backdrop to his press conferences, we
knew we were a little bit freer. When Bree Newsome climbed up a
South Carolina flagpole and yanked that Confederate flag down, we
felt a little freer. And when the respected Southern-based organizer
Mary Hooks told us, as only she could, to pool our dollars, to use
them as crowbars to pry open the steel cages and free our sisters
during the Black Mama's Bail Out campaign, we all felt a little freer.
Acts of defiance, disruption, and insurgent rule breaking are ways
that we delink from the politics of routine, of acclimation, of com-
promise, and of collaboration. To paraphrase James Baldwin, it is
when we demand the impossible that we come close to real
freedom.

What do I see when I look at this cohort of activists? I see the
faces of thirteen-year-olds who peered out the narrow windows
at the Juvenile Detention Center to see hundreds of young activists marching through the chilly Chicago night holding up signs
saying "We love you." I see you on ladders wrapped in chains,
holding flags and banners. I see you daringly wading out into
rush hour traffic on major highways to force people to look at the

reality of Black death, determined in the spirit of "No pasaran." I
see Josh and Jasmine peering from behind cold steel bars, and I
see MarShawn dead on the steps of the Ohio statehouse. I see
you crying quietly at the back of the church during Alton Ster-
ling's funeral and standing alongside Eric's daughter, Tamir's
mother, Rekia's brother. I see you in a hot, crowded little house
in Havana, drinking beer and talking politics in two languages;
in a dusty refugee camp near Ramallah; in a favela in Rio after
meeting with the Landless Workers Movement, comparing notes
about displacement; and in a shantytown outside Joburg trying to
make sense of a revolution gone astray. Above all, I hear you
insisting this is a world family, and the struggle goes far beyond
the borders that the colonizers carved out in the earth. And even
when we disagree, we are dancing the same dance.

Finally, I see you building political altars, paying homage to
the wisdom of grandmothers and grandfathers, knowing all the
while that your eyes will witness, and your hands will build, a
world they could only have imagined. When you chant, "We
know that we will win," in a spiraling crescendo, I believe you. I
believe you with love, hope, and expectation all wrapped around
you in a fierce and unrelenting embrace.

ACKNOWLEDGMENTS

If an author has done her or his due diligence, there are always more people to thank than time and space can fairly afford. This is especially true when writing about a social movement in progress. When I ask amazing organizers to take time out of their work to sit and talk with me, they are giving a gift of trust. They are also investing in the future in ways none of us fully appreciates in the moment. I am enormously grateful and honored to have the opportunity to tell this story, a story that is undoubtedly incomplete, and perhaps contains an unintended mistake or two, for which I take full credit. As I have jokingly said in the course of writing this book, as a historian I am used to writing about the lives of dead people. My previous subjects have usually said and done all that they were going to say and do. In contrast, the organizers in the Movement for Black Lives are very alive and therefore are moving targets for any analyses or neat summaries that might attempt to pin them down. This is compounded by the fact that I know, respect, and have genuine affection for many of them. But as my dear friend the great historian John Dittmer and I once said to each other, we have to love our subjects enough to tell the truth about them. So I have tried to do just that. I have not told all that I know about the movement—a writer never does. Rather, we curate a set of narratives that we feel convey to the reader the most important and salient information that will frame and explain the essence of the subject. That has been my goal.

Those who have helped me in this effort, with patience and generosity, include all of those listed in the bibliography as interviewees, as well as others who have served as readers, critics, editors, fact checkers, cheerleaders, advisors, and sources of inspiration. Without spelling out the unique role each person has played in the production of this book, I offer a large and heartfelt expression of thanks to my beloveds, colleagues, comrades, family, friends, and research assistants: M. Adams, Jen Ash, Bill Ayers, Martha Biondi, Janae Bonsu, Maxx Boykins, Adam Bush, Rosi Carasco, Charlene Carruthers, Cathy J. Cohen, Brian Colar, Kristiana Rae Colón, Dara Cooper, Angela Y. Davis, Gina Dent, Bernardine Dohrn, Joan Fadayiro, Roderick Ferguson, Bill Fletcher Jr., Alicia Garza, Adom Getachew, Keedra Gibba, Brianna Gibson, Rachel Gilmer, Bill Gladstone, Dayo Gore, Beverly Guy-Sheftall, Sarah Haley, Paris Hatcher, Ash-Lee Henderson, Lynette Jackson, Mariame Kaba, Robin D. G. Kelley, Patrisse Khan-Cullors, Alice Kim, Lisa Yun Lee, Ntanya Lee, Deana Lewis, Karissa Lewis, Tamika Lewis, Page May, Essence McDowell, Thenjiwe McHarris, Moe Mitchell, Chandra Talpade Mohanty, Leith Mullings, Nadine Naber, Premilla Nadasen, Prexy Nesbitt, Leena and Camille Odeh, Jasson Perez, Denise Perry, Asha Ransby-Sporn, Beth E. Richie, Andrea Ritchie, Jamala Rogers, Angie Rollins (Fresco Steez), Atef Said, C. Riley Snorton, Todd St. Hill, Jan Susler, Stacey Sutton, Keeanga-Yamahtta Taylor, Makani Themba, James Thindwa, Opal Tometi, Ayoka Turner, Martin Unzueta, Simeko Washington, and many more. A huge gratitude to each of the thirty-nine people listed in the bibliography, who made time to be interviewed.

I thank Lisa Duggan and Curtis Marez for inviting and encouraging me to write this book. I thank Niels Hooper for his enormous patience as an editor, as this project suffered delay after delay owing to my other political and professional obligations. Thanks to the entire University of California Press staff, especially Kate Hoffman. And big thanks to Noor Shawaf for her top-notch editorial skills and her calm amid the storm. I appreciate my amazing collection of colleagues at the University of Illinois at Chicago in African American studies, gender and women's studies, and history; my co-workers at the Social Justice Initiative; and my coconspirators at the *Souls* journal, the Woods Fund, the National Women's Studies Association, the "Resist. Reimagine. Rebuild" and The Majority coalitions, and the journal *Race and Class* (and in loving remembrance of Siva, founder of the journal, who represented the very best of what it means to fulfill the obligations of a Black radical intellectual).

And then there is my dear partner for over thirty-five years, Peter Sporn. You support me in all I do. And I am proud of all that you do. You have been a doctor to the masses, and most of our close friends and comrades have called upon you for one health concern or another, because of your enormous grace and generosity in the face of suffering. I am grateful for our children, Jason and Asha, both of whom represent, in their own distinct areas of work, great hope for the future. Thank you both for making us proud and bringing such light into our lives. I acknowledge the rest of my family, including my extended family, and dear friends, who have lent inspiration and support in various ways: Pam, Pablo, Papito, Lisa, Lelanie, Josh, Dara, Diane Martin, Beverly Rice, Jannye Manning, Kim Byas Sr., Tracye Matthews, Kim Smith, Michelle Lawrence, Iasha and Elena Sznajder, Brianna Gibson, Dara Reiff, the entire Martin family, and Mr. Charles Cohen. And thank you to Ella Cohen-Richie, who will one day read her Auntie Barbara's books and will understand why, along with her amazing moms, I have so much hope for what she too will give to the world and toward the liberation of our people, and all people. Finally, I am grateful to the family that raised me (all of whom are now passed on): Ethel and Charlie Ransby and Rosia Lee and Henry Pittman. They had very little, gave a great deal, and asked simply for decency, fairness, and justice in return. We fight for a world in which all that they asked for will be realized for everyone.

Royalties from this book will be contributed to further racial and social justice work.

NOTES

EPIGRAPH

Patrisse Khan-Cullors, interview by Christina Heatherton, *Policing the Planet: Why the Policing Crisis Led to Black Lives Matter,* eds. Jordan T. Camp and Christina Heatherton (New York: Verso Books, 2016).

INTRODUCTION

1. Juliana Menasce Horowitz and Gretchen Livingston, "How Americans View the Black Lives Matter Movement," Pew Research Center, July 8, 2016, www.pewresearch.org/fact-tank/2016/07/08/how-americans-view-the-black-lives-matter-movement/.

2. Deen Freelon, Charlton D. McIlwain, and Meredith D. Clark, *Beyond the Hashtags: #Ferguson, #BlackLivesMatter, and the Online Struggle for Offline Justice* (report, Center for Media and Social Impact, School of Communication, American University, 2016), 33–34, http://archive .cmsimpact.org/sites/default/files/beyond_the_hashtags_2016.pdf.

3. *Intersectionality* is an intellectual and political framework and practice that recognizes the simultaneity and interrelated nature of various systems of oppression—namely, racism, sexism, capitalism, imperialism, ableism, and hetero-patriarchy. It is a term that was

coined by critical race theory scholar Kimberlé Crenshaw in 1989; see Kimberlé Crenshaw, "Demarginalizing the Intersection of Race and Sex: A Black Feminist Critique of Antidiscrimination Doctrine, Feminist Theory and Antiracist Politics," *University of Chicago Legal Forum* 1 (1989): 139–67.

The concept, however, had been at the core of Black female organizing and scholarship long before, as reflected in Third World Women's Alliance's Frances Beal's *Triple Jeopardy in CRCS;* and Angela Y. Davis, *Women, Race, and Class* (New York: Random House, 1981). It can really be traced to Sojourner Truth's "Ain't I a Woman?" speech, delivered to the Women's Convention, Akron, Ohio, December 1851.

4. It should be noted that some St. Louis activists do not embrace the Black Lives Matter moniker, arguing that the Ferguson uprising was not organized by the founders of #BLM and that "Black Live Matter" was not the only chant on the streets during the rebellion. There have also been critiques about the ways in which the media's focus on #BLM and its three founders has lessened the emphasis on the leaders of the street protests in Ferguson.

5. Freelon, McIlwain, and Clark, *Beyond the Hashtags,* 42–43.

6. Michael McLaughlin, "The Dynamic History of #BlackLivesMatter Explained," *Huffington Post,* updated December 26, 2016, www.huffingtonpost.com/entry/history-black-lives-matter_us_56d0a3b0e4b0871f60eb4af5.

7. The term *neoliberalism* is used quite commonly but has competing definitions. I offer the following working definition for purposes of understanding its usage in this book: First advanced in the nineteenth century, it currently refers to privatization, deregulation, and a kind of laissez-faire capitalism, according to which the government plays a minimal role and the free market supposedly governs the economy. Milton Friedman is closely associated with neoliberal policies, such as those he advised the Pinochet government to implement in Chile after the US-backed coup that ousted the democratically elected president Salvador Allende. David Harvey, Marxist geographer and critic of neoliberalism, views it as the capitalist instrumentalization of politics. In a neoliberal frame the market is supreme.

8. "About," Black Lives Matter Global Network, https://black livesmatter.com/about/.

9. Million Hoodies Movement for Justice is no longer part of the M4BL coalition.

10. Aldon D. Morris, *The Origins of the Civil Rights Movement: Black Communities Organizing for Change* (New York: Free Press, 1984).

11. Haeyoun Park and Jasmine C. Lee, "Looking for Accountability in Police-Involved Deaths of Blacks," *New York Times,* updated May 3, 2017, www.nytimes.com/interactive/2016/07/12/us/looking-for-accountability-in-police-involved-deaths-of-blacks.html.

CHAPTER ONE. ROOTS AND RECALIBRATED EXPECTATIONS

1. Cathy J. Cohen, *The Boundaries of Blackness: AIDS and the Breakdown of Black Politics* (Chicago: University of Chicago Press, 1999).

2. M. Adams, email interview with the author, March 6, 2018.

3. See "The Black Radical Congress: A Black Freedom Agenda for the Twenty-First Century," *Black Scholar* 28, no. 1 (1998): 71–73.

4. Based on the author's firsthand experience in planning meetings and conversations, and on an original document of the Black Radical Congress's founding principles in the author's possession.

5. Following are examples of BRC members serving in supportive and generative capacities with respect to BLMM/M4BL: Cathy Cohen helped to launch BYP100; Cornel West was repeatedly arrested alongside Ferguson protestors; Robin D.G. Kelley, Barbara Ransby, Bill Fletcher Jr., Cathy Cohen, Angela Davis, and Lisa Brock have been sought out for advice; Jamala Rogers, known as "Mama Jamala," was an anchor for the Ferguson protests and a mentor to the leaders' new groups that sprung up out of it.

6. "About," Critical Resistance, http://criticalresistance.org/about/; "The History of Critical Resistance," *Social Justice* 27, no. 3 (2000): 6–10; Angela Y. Davis, "Masked Racism: Reflections on the Prison Industrial Complex," *Colorlines,* September 10, 1998, www.colorlines.com/articles /masked-racism-reflections-prison-industrial-complex.

7. "Analysis," INCITE!, www.incite-national.org/page/analysis.

8. INCITE! Women of Color against Violence, *Color of Violence: The INCITE! Anthology* (Cambridge, MA: South End Press, 2006; repr., Durham: Duke University Press, 2016); INCITE! Women of Color against Violence, *The Revolution Will Not Be Funded: Beyond the Non-profit Industrial Complex* (Cambridge, MA: South End Press, 2007; repr., Durham: Duke University Press, 2017); Beth E. Richie, *Arrested Justice: Black Women, Violence, and America's Prison Nation* (New York: New York University Press, 2012); Ruth Wilson Gilmore, *Golden Gulag* (Berkeley: University of California Press, 2007); Angela Y. Davis, *Are Prisons Obsolete?* (New York: Seven Stories Press, 2003).

9. Richie, *Arrested Justice.*

10. Michelle Alexander, *The New Jim Crow: Mass Incarceration in the Age of Colorblindness,* 2nd ed. (New York: New Press, 2012), 189–90, 22–23.

11. Angela Y. Davis, *Freedom Is a Constant Struggle: Ferguson, Palestine, and the Foundations of a Movement* (Chicago: Haymarket Books, 2016), 36.

12. Davis, *Freedom,* 82.

13. Eddie S. Glaude Jr., *Democracy in Black: How Race Still Enslaves the American Soul* (New York: Broadway Books, 2016); Tavis Smiley, ed., *The Covenant with Black America—Ten Years Later* (Carlsbad, CA: Smiley Books, 2016); Michael Eric Dyson, *The Black Presidency: Barack Obama and the Politics of Race in America* (New York: Houghton Mifflin Harcourt, 2016); Frederick C. Harris, *The Price of the Ticket: Barack Obama and the Rise and Decline of Black Politics* (New York: Oxford University Press, 2012).

14. Jelani Cobb, "The Matter of Black Lives," *New Yorker,* March 14, 2016, www.newyorker.com/magazine/2016/03/14/where-is-black-lives-matter-headed.

15. "Black Power: A Q & A with Charlene Carruthers," Black Youth Project, February 11, 2016, http://blackyouthproject.com/black-power-a-qa-with-charlene-carruthers/.

16. Tef Poe, "Dear Mr. President: A Letter from Tef Poe," *Riverfront Times,* December 1, 2014, www.riverfronttimes.com/musicblog/2014/12/01/dear-mr-president-a-letter-from-tef-poe?page=2.

17. See Lfe Johari Uhuru, "'Occupy the Hood': Including All of the 99%," interview by Jesse Strauss, *Al Jazeera,* October 10, 2011, www .aljazeera.com/indepth/features/2011/10/20111091910197087867.html.

18. Initially chapters were allowed to form and determine their own membership rules. Later the national leadership and staff set parameters so that there was some consistency.

19. Keeanga-Yamahtta Taylor, *From #BlackLivesMatter to Black Liberation* (Chicago: Haymarket Books, 2016), 144–48.

20. Cobb, "Matter of Black Lives."

21. Charlene Carruthers, phone interview with the author, February 15, 2017; Charlene Carruthers, "Not Your Grandfather's Black Freedom Movement: An Interview with BYP100's Charlene Carruthers," by Salim Muwakkil, *In These Times,* February 8, 2016, http://inthesetimes .com/article/18755/charlene-carruthers-on-byp200-Laquan-McDonald-and-police-violence.

22. Opal Tometi, email interview with the author, November 21, 2017.

23. Tometi, interview.

24. Biographical information for Patrisse Khan-Cullors is from a phone interview with the author, April 11, 2017; Abby Sewell, "Activists Battle L.A. County Jailers' 'Culture of Violence,'" *Los Angeles Times,* April 14, 2014, www.latimes.com/local/la-me-c1-jail-activist-20140414-m-story.html.

CHAPTER TWO. JUSTICE FOR TRAYVON

1. Richard Luscombe, "Jury Hears Emotional Opening Statements in George Zimmerman Trial," *Guardian,* June 24, 2013, www.theguardian .com/world/2013/jun/24/george-zimmerman-trial-opening-statements.

2. Washington Post Staff, "President Obama's Remarks on Trayvon Martin (Full Transcript)," *Washington Post,* July 19, 2013, www.washing tonpost.com/politics/president-obamas-remarks-on-trayvon-martin-full-transcript/2013/07/19/5e33ebea-f09a-11e2-a1f9-ea873b7e0424_story .html.

3. Ryan Devereaux, "Echoes of Trayvon Martin as Residents Seek Justice for Bronx Teen's Death," *Guardian,* March 30, 2012, www

.theguardian.com/world/2012/mar/30/trayvon-martin-ramarley-graham-bronx-teenager; Associated Press, "Trayvon Martin Death: Thousands March in Town Where Teenager Was Shot," *Guardian,* March 31, 2012, www.theguardian.com/world/2012/mar/31/trayvon-martin-protest-march-sanford; Trymaine Lee, "Trayvon Martin Case Protests across Nation Culminate with Show of Strength in Florida," *Huffington Post,* March 23, 2012, www.huffingtonpost.com/2012/03/23/trayvon-martin-rally-national-protest_n_1375699.html.

4. There were other protest movements against racism, including the 2006–7 mass protests in support of the Jena Six, a group of Black high school students in Louisiana prosecuted for attempted murder after a fight with a white classmate and in an atmosphere in which white students had hung nooses from nearby trees to simulate lynching. See Amy Waldman, "The Truth about Jena," *Atlantic,* January/February 2008.

5. Michelle Ye Hee Lee, "The Viral Claim That a Black Person Is Killed by Police Every 28 Hours," *Washington Post,* December 24, 2014, www.washingtonpost.com/news/fact-checker/wp/2014/12/24/the-viral-claim-that-a-black-person-is-killed-by-police-every-28-hours/; "Fatal Force," *Washington Post,* www.washingtonpost.com/graphics/2018/national/police-shootings-201.

6. Michelle Alexander, "Why Hillary Clinton Doesn't Deserve the Black Vote," *Nation,* February 10, 2016.

7. Phillip Agnew is sometimes referred to as Umi Selah but, as of the writing of this book, chooses to use the name Phillip Agnew.

8. Rachel Gilmer, email interview with the author, August 14, 2017.

9. Gilmer, interview.

10. Gilmer, interview.

11. Sarah Jaffe, "Young Activists Occupy Florida Capitol, Demand Justice for Trayvon," *In These Times,* July 25, 2013, http://inthesetimes.com/article/15356/young_activists_occupy_florida_capitol_demand_justice_for_trayvon.

12. Kristian Davis Bailey, "Dream Defenders, Black Lives Matter & Ferguson Reps Take Historic Trip to Palestine," *Ebony,* January 9, 2015, www.ebony.com/news-views/dream-defenders-black-lives-matter-ferguson-reps-take-historic-trip-to-palestine#axzz46CjFClpZ.

13. "About," Dream Defenders, www.dreamdefenders.org/about.

14. Gilmer, interview.

15. Jessica Pierce, comments from "Opening Roundtable: The Long Struggle for Civil Rights and Black Freedom," Future of the African American Past conference, cohosted by the American Historical Association and the Smithsonian National Museum of African American History and Culture, Washington, DC, May 19, 2016.

16. Darryl Holliday, "The New Black Power," *Chicago Magazine,* February 22, 2016, www.chicagomag.com/Chicago-Magazine/March-2016/black-leaders.

17. For Carruthers's reflections on her role in BYP100, see her *Unapologetic: A Black, Queer and Feminist Mandate for Our Movement* (Boston: Beacon Press, forthcoming).

18. Cohen introduced the BYP100 project to Arcus, from which it received its first grant, allowing the new group to hire Carruthers and begin to organize full time. See "The BYP Hires Charlene Carruthers as the National Coordinator of the BYP 100," Black Youth Project, November 6, 2013, http://blackyouthproject.com/the-byp-hires-charlene-carruthers-as-the-national-coordinator-of-the-byp-100/.

19. Asha Ransby-Sporn, email interview with the author, February 8, 2017.

20. Author's observation and participation.

21. Mariame Kaba, email interview with the author, October 23, 2017.

22. "SisterSong and Free Marissa Now Joining Forces for Standing Our Ground," *North Dallas Gazette,* July 16, 2014, https://northdallasgazette.com/2014/07/16/sistersong-and-free-marissa-now-joining-forces-for-standing-our-ground/; Monica Simpson, "Standing Our Ground: Reproductive Justice for Marissa Alexander," *Rewire.News,* April 18, 2014, https://rewire.news/article/2014/04/18/standing-ground-reproductive-justice-marissa-alexander/.

23. As of January 2017, Alexander had been released from all restrictions. Her conviction has still not been expunged from her record. See Christine Hauser, "Florida Woman Whose 'Stand Your Ground' Defense Was Rejected Is Released," *New York Times,* February 7, 2017,

www.nytimes.com/2017/02/07/us/marissa-alexander-released-stand-your-ground.html.

CHAPTER THREE. THE FERGUSON UPRISING AND ITS REVERBERATIONS

1. US Department of Justice, *Department of Justice Report Regarding the Criminal Investigation into the Shooting Death of Michael Brown by Ferguson, Missouri Police Officer Darren Wilson*, memorandum, March 4, 2015, www.justice.gov/sites/default/files/opa/press-releases/attachments/2015/03/04/doj_report_on_shooting_of_michael_brown_1.pdf; Terrence McCoy, "Darren Wilson Explains Why He Killed Michael Brown," *Washington Post*, November 25, 2014, www.washingtonpost.com/news/morning-mix/wp/2014/11/25/why-darren-wilson-said-he-killed-michael-brown/.

2. Lezley McSpadden, *Tell the Truth & Shame the Devil: The Life, Legacy, and Love of My Son Michael Brown* (New York, Regan Arts, 2016), 5.

3. Matt Apuzzo, "Ferguson Police Routinely Violate Rights of Blacks, Justice Dept. Finds," *New York Times*, March 3, 2015.

4. Racial capitalism, as articulated by Cedric Robinson, and expanded upon by Robin D. G. Kelley, Ruth Gilmore, and others, can be defined simply as a view of capitalism that recognizes its inextricable links to white supremacy as manifest in genocide, settler colonialism, slavery, empire building, and the racial regimes that followed, including Jim Crow segregation and, more recently, racialized mass incarceration. See Cedric Robinson, *Black Marxism: The Making of the Black Radical Tradition* (Chapel Hill: University of North Carolina Press, 2000); Robin D. G. Kelley, "What Did Cedric Robinson Mean by Racial Capitalism?," *Boston Review*, January 12, 2017; Ruth Wilson Gilmore, *Golden Gulag: Prisons, Surplus, Crisis, and Opposition in Globalizing California* (Berkeley: University of California Press, 2007).

5. Marc Lamont Hill, *Nobody: Casualties of America's War on the Vulnerable, from Ferguson to Flint and Beyond* (New York: Atria Books, 2016), xix–xx.

6. Spencer Ackerman, "US Police Given Billions from Homeland Security for 'Tactical' Equipment," *Guardian*, August 20, 2014, www

.theguardian.com/world/2014/aug/20/police-billions-homeland-security-military-equipment.

7. See Sebastian Murdock and Andres Jauregui, "Cop Ray Albers in Ferguson to Protestors: 'I Will F**king Kill You,'" *Huffington Post,* August 20, 2014, www.huffingtonpost.com/2014/08/20/ferguson-cop-i-will-kill-you_n_5695748.html; Arit John, "Ferguson Police Arrest Two Reporters Who Tried to Film Them in a McDonald's," *Atlantic,* August 13, 2014, www.theatlantic.com/politics/archive/2014/08/ferguson-police-arrested-reporters-from-the-washington-post-and-huffington-post/376050/; Max Fisher, "If Police in Ferguson Treat Journalists like This, Imagine How They Treat Residents," *Vox,* August 18, 2014, www.vox.com/2014/8/18/6043247/ferguson-police-media-harassment.

8. Brittany Ferrell, phone interview with the author, November 10, 2017.

9. Ferrell, interview.

10. Ferrell, interview.

11. Ferrell, interview.

12. Kayla Reed, phone interview with the author, November 6, 2017.

13. Reed, interview.

14. Reed, interview.

15. Reed, interview.

16. Tim Pool, "Ferguson: A Report from Occupied Territory," *Fusion,* March 30, 2015, on YouTube, 53:22, www.youtube.com/watch?v=gq9pHONmaLc.

17. Jamilah Lemieux, "[Ferguson Forward] Montague Simmons and OBS: Revolutionary Re-Up," *Ebony,* August 8, 2015, www.ebony.com/news-views/ferguson-forward-montague-simmons-and-obs-revolutionary-re-up-403.

18. Rasheed Aldridge, interview with the author, St. Louis, Missouri, March 11, 2016.

19. Aldridge, interview.

20. Julia Ho and Elizabeth Vega, interview with the author, St. Louis, Missouri, March 12, 2016.

21. Mallory Nezam, "Ferguson and the Art of Protest," *Mantle,* February 9, 2015, www.mantlethought.org/arts-and-culture/ferguson-art-

protest; "About," The Mirror Casket Project, http://mirrorcasket.com /aboutus; Associated Press and Snejana Farberov, "Demonstrators Chanting 'Killer Cops' Carry a Mirrored Coffin through the Streets of Ferguson as 100 Police in Riot Gear Form a Line to Face Them Down," *Daily Mail,* October 11, 2014, www.dailymail.co.uk/news/article-2789204/ferguson-demonstrators-chanting-killer-cops-use-mirrored-coffin-make-statement-ahead-weekend-protests.html.

22. Nabeegah Azeri, interview with the author, St. Louis, Missouri, March 12, 2016.

23. Kristiana Rae Colón, "Showdown at Beauty Town," *Lost Voices* (blog), October 1, 2014, www.thelostvoices.org/blog (site discontinued).

24. For more information, visit the Hands Up United website: www.handsupunited.org.

25. See "The People's Pantry," Hands Up United, www.handsupunited .org/peoplespantry/.

26. Jon Swaine, "Ferguson Protester Faces Four Years' Jail over Charges of Kicking SUV," *Guardian,* August 12, 2015, www.theguardian .com/us-news/2015/aug/13/ferguson-protester-faces-four-years-jail-over-charges-of-attacking-suv-and-driver.

27. Sunnivie Brydum, "Watch: 'We Don't Want Reform, We Want Revolution,'" *Advocate,* February 7, 2015, www.advocate.com/politics /2015/02/07/watch-we-dont-want-reform-we-want-revolution; see also Brittany Ferrell and Alexis Templeton, "[Ferguson Forward] Brittany and Alexis: In Love and Struggle," interview by Jamilah Lemieux, *Ebony,* August 7, 2015, www.ebony.com/news-views/ferguson-forward-brittany-and-alexis-in-love-and-struggle-404.

28. Gabrielle Korn, "This Is What It's Like to Be a Youth Activist in Ferguson," *Nylon,* December 2, 2014, www.nylon.com/articles/brittany-ferrell-interview. See also Erica Caldwell, "Where My Girls At: Meet Two of Ferguson's Black Queer Activists," *Bitch Media,* April 27, 2015, www.bitchmedia.org/post/where-my-girls-at-meet-fergusons-black-queer-activists.

29. Darnell L. Moore, "Black Freedom Fighters in Ferguson: Some of Us Are Queer," *Feminist Wire,* October, 17, 2014, www .thefeministwire.com/2014/10/some-of-us-are-queer.

30. Sarah van Gelder, "Rev. Sekou on Today's Civil Rights Leaders: 'I Take My Orders from 23-Year-Old Queer Women,'" *YES! Magazine*, July 22, 2015, www.yesmagazine.org/peace-justice/black-lives-matter-s-favorite-minister-reverend-sekou-young-queer.

31. See Bene Viera, "How Activist (and ESSENCE Cover Star) Johnetta 'Netta' Elzie Speaks Her Truth and What It's Like Fighting for Yours," *Essence*, January 6, 2016, www.essence.com/2016/01/06/how-activist-and-essence-cover-star-johnetta-netta-elzie-speaks-her-truth-and-what-its.

32. Noah Berlatsky, "The Women of #BlackLivesMatter," *Atlantic*, January 27, 2015, www.theatlantic.com/national/archive/2015/01/women-and-blacklivesmatter/384855/.

33. Berlatsky, "Women of #BlackLivesMatter."

34. Berlatsky, "Women of #BlackLivesMatter." It should be noted that Johnetta Elzie posted a harshly critical indictment of the 2017 Women's March on Washington (and sister marches) in the form of a poem in *Teen Vogue* that asked angrily where the marchers during the Black Lives Matter protests had been. See Johnetta Elzie, "A Poem about the Women's March by Johnetta Elzie," *Teen Vogue*, January 23, 2017, www.teenvogue.com/story/a-poem-by-johnetta-elzie.

35. Alisha Sonnier, interview with the author, St. Louis, Missouri, March 12, 2016.

36. Sonnier, interview.

37. Sonnier, interview.

38. Sonnier, interview; Nathan Rubbelke, "Saint Louis University to Erect Monument Honoring Anti-police Protest," *College Fix*, February 3, 2015, www.thecollegefix.com/post/21099/.

39. Sonnier, interview.

40. Sonnier, interview.

41. Sonnier, interview.

42. Sonnier, interview.

43. Sonnier, interview.

44. Sonnier, interview. Note the Daniel Holtzclaw case, discussed in chapter 5, in which an Oklahoma City police officer was convicted of raping and sodomizing women in his custody.

45. US Department of Justice, *Investigation of Ferguson Police Department*, Civil Rights Division, March 4, 2015, www.justice.gov/sites /default/files/opa/press-releases/attachments/2015/03/04/ferguson_ police_department_report.pdf.

46. Jamala Rogers, *Ferguson Is America: Roots of Rebellion* (Mira Digital, 2015), x.

47. For information on and a critique of broken windows policing, see Bernard E. Harcourt, *Illusion of Order: The False Promise of Broken Windows Policing* (Cambridge, MA: Harvard University Press, 2001).

48. Historian Evelyn Brooks Higginbotham first coined the term *politics of respectability*, but in a very specific way, to refer to a strategy used by middle-class Black women in the late nineteenth and early twentieth centuries to advance racial progress and simultaneously shield themselves and others from scurrilous attacks on their dignity and humanity. A byproduct of this approach, however, has been to "police" the behavior of those poor, working-class members of the race who were unwilling or unable to conform to the dictates of respectability. For an example of media debate about how to view looters in the context of the rebellion, see Van Jones taking on Don Lemon in Ferguson over the nature of the protests, in Evan McMurry, "CNN's Jones, Lemon Rip into Each Other over Ferguson Protests," *Mediaite*, November 25, 2014, www.mediaite.com/tv/cnns-jones-lemon-rip-into-each-other-over-ferguson-protests/.

49. Fredrick C. Harris, "The Rise of Respectability Politics," *Dissent*, Winter 2014, www.dissentmagazine.org/article/the-rise-of-respectability-politics/.

50. Maurice (Moe) Mitchell (@ciphersankofa), "No hyperbole. No exaggeration. This is a war zone. Why is are [*sic*] government so intent on silencing these young people?," Twitter, August 17, 2014, https:// twitter.com/ciphersankofa/status/501207323822817280.

51. Mark Molloy and Agencies, "Palestinians Tweet Tear Gas Advice to Protesters in Ferguson," *Telegraph*, August 15, 2014, www .telegraph.co.uk/news/worldnews/northamerica/usa/11036190/Palestinians-tweet-tear-gas-advice-to-protesters-in-Ferguson.html.

52. Rogers, *Ferguson Is America*, 78.

53. Marisa Franco, "Latino Communities Must See Ferguson's Fight as Their Own," MSNBC, August 20, 2014, www.msnbc.com /melissa-harris-perry/latino-communities-must-see-fergusons-fight-their-own.

54. See Sharita Gruberg, "How For-Profit Companies Are Driving Immigration Detention Policies," *Center for American Progress,* December 18, 2015, www.americanprogress.org/issues/immigration/reports /2015/12/18/127769/how-for-profit-companies-are-driving-immigration-detention-policies/.

55. Service Employees International Union, "Statement of SEIU President Mary Kay Henry on the Grand Jury Decision in Ferguson, Missouri," November 24, 2014, www.seiu.org/2014/11/statement-of-seiu-president-mary-kay-henry-on-the.

56. "About," Black Lives Matter Global Network, https://black livesmatter.com/about/.

57. Alicia Garza, "A Herstory of the #BlackLivesMatter Movement," *Feminist Wire,* October 7, 2014, www.thefeministwire.com/2014 /10/blacklivesmatter-2/.

58. Seung Min Kim, "Black Lives Matter Pushes Back on Ohio Senate Endorsement," *Politico,* July 29, 2016, www.politico.com/story /2016/07/black-lives-matter-rob-portman-226436.

59. The Blackbird collective moved to institutionalize the Movement for Black Lives with the constituent organizations that came together to convene the conference. The group has organized itself into several "tables" or committees, including the policy table, action table, and strategy table.

60. Ash-Lee Henderson, email interview with the author, March 10, 2018.

61. John Eligon and Richard Pérez-Peña, "University of Missouri Protests Spur a Day of Change," *New York Times,* November 9, 2105, www.nytimes.com/2015/11/10/us/university-of-missouri-system-president-resigns.html?_r=0; and conversations with Jennifer Pagan, former student at Mizzou, December 1, 2017, Chicago.

62. "About," Black Liberation Collective, www.blackliberation collective.org.

CHAPTER FOUR. BLACK RAGE AND BLACKS
IN POWER

1. See Mark Binelli, "The Fire Last Time," *New Republic,* April 6, 2017, https://newrepublic.com/article/141701/fire-last-time-detroit-stress-police-squad-terrorized-black-community. This article does not give its sources.

2. Mosby prosecuted the six officers implicated in Gray's death. She was then sued by five of the officers for "malicious prosecution," after jury trials failed to convict them. See Justin Fenton, "Freddie Gray Case: Judge Allows Malicious Prosecution Lawsuit against Mosby to Proceed," *Baltimore Sun,* January 6, 2017, www.baltimoresun.com/news/maryland/freddie-gray/bs-md-ci-mosby-lawsuit-to-proceed-20170106-story.html.

3. Mychal Denzel Smith, "The Rebirth of Black Rage," *Nation,* August 13, 2015, www.thenation.com/article/the-rebirth-of-black-rage.

4. Brittney Cooper, "In Defense of Black Rage: Michael Brown, Police and the American Dream," *Salon,* August 12, 2014, www.salon.com/2014/08/12/in_defense_of_black_rage_michael_brown_police_and_the_american_dream.

5. Martin Luther King Jr., "Beyond Vietnam," speech given at the Riverside Church, New York, on April 4, 1967, in Clayborne Carson and Kris Shepard, eds., *A Call to Conscience: The Landmark Speeches of Dr. Martin Luther King, Jr.* (New York: Hachette, 2001), 79.

6. "BYP100 in Defense of Black Rage and Black Resistance," BYP100, July 8, 2016, http://byp100.org/byp100-in-defense-of-black-rage-and-black-resistance.

7. Dayvon Love, phone interview with the author, November 6, 2017.

8. Dave Zirin, "Makayla Gilliam-Price and Baltimore's Debt to a Remarkable Family," *Nation,* May 1, 2015, www.thenation.com/article/makayla-gilliam-price-and-baltimores-debt-remarkable-family/.

9. Kenrya Rankin, "Baltimore Activists Protest Police Commissioner Appointment, Arrested during Sit-In," *Colorlines,* October 15, 2015, www.colorlines.com/articles/baltimore-activists-protest-police-commissioner-appointment-arrested-during-sit; Kevin Rector and

Colin Campbell, "Protesters Occupy City Hall after Kevin Davis' Appointment Hearing," *Baltimore Sun,* October 15, 2015, www.baltimoresun.com/news/maryland/baltimore-city/bs-md-ci-davis-confirmation-hearing-20151014-story.html.

10. Love, interview.

11. Jean Marbella, "Beginning of Freddie Gray's Life as Sad as Its End, Court Case Shows," *Baltimore Sun,* April 23, 2015, www.baltimoresun.com/news/maryland/baltimore-city/bs-md-freddie-gray-lead-paint-20150423-story.html.

12. Dayvon Love, "Continuing Activism after the Cameras Leave," interview by Melissa Harris-Perry, *Melissa Harris-Perry Show,* aired May 2, 2015, on MSNBC, www.msnbc.com/melissa-harris-perry/watch/continuing-activism-after-the-cameras-leave-438306883710.

13. Justin Fenton, "Tyrone West Files Show Passenger's Account of Death in Police Custody," *Baltimore Sun,* January 23, 2014, http://articles.baltimoresun.com/2014-01-23/news/bs-md-ci-tyrone-west-witness-20140122_1_tyrone-west-jorge-bernardez-ruiz-kitmore-road; Justin Fenton, "Independent Review Faults City Police in Tyrone West Case," *Baltimore Sun,* August 8, 2014, http://articles.baltimoresun.com/2014-08-08/news/bs-md-ci-tyrone-west-outside-review-20140808_1_tyrone-west-james-chips-stewart-excessive-force.

14. Michaela Brown, email interview with the author, December 15, 2017.

15. US Department of Justice, *Investigation of the Baltimore City Police Department,* Civil Rights Division, August 10, 2016, www.justice.gov/opa/file/883366/download, 122–26.

16. Jessica Anderson and Christiana Amarachi Mbakwe, "Korryn Gaines Was Passionate about Beliefs, Anticipated Violent Confrontation with Police," *Baltimore Sun,* August 5, 2016, www.baltimoresun.com/news/maryland/crime/bs-md-co-korryn-gaines-profile-20160804-story.html.

17. Anderson and Mbakwe, "Korryn Gaines."

18. Anderson and Mbakwe, "Korryn Gaines."

19. Courtney Sherwood and Kirk Johnson, "Bundy Brothers Acquitted in Takeover of Oregon Wildlife Refuge," *New York Times,*

October 27, 2016, www.nytimes.com/2016/10/28/us/bundy-brothers-acquitted-in-takeover-of-oregon-wildlife-refuge.html?_r=0.

20. Driadonna Roland, "Sovereign Law Made Cliven Bundy a 'Patriot' but Korryn Gaines 'Crazy,'" *Revolt,* August 8, 2016, https://revolt.tv/stories/2016/08/08/sovereign-law-made-cliven-bundy-patriot-korryn-gaines-crazy-3517d33d30.

21. See Charlene Carruthers, "In Defense of Korryn Gaines, Black Women and Children," *Colorlines,* August 5, 2016, www.colorlines.com/articles/defense-korryn-gaines-black-women-and-children-opinion.

22. BLMGN actually hired a person to work full-time on healing justice. BYP100 has a healing and accountability committee.

23. Jonathan Capehart, "Marilyn Mosby's Amazing Press Conference," *Washington Post,* May 1, 2015, www.washingtonpost.com/blogs/post-partisan/wp/2015/05/01/marilyn-mosbys-amazing-press-conference.

24. Wil S. Hylton, "Baltimore vs. Marilyn Mosby," *New York Times Magazine,* September 28, 2016.

25. US Department of Justice, *Investigation of the Baltimore City Police Department,* Civil Rights Division, August 10, 2016, www.justice.gov/opa/file/883366/download, 98.

26. DeRay McKesson, acting as an individual, endorsed Hillary Clinton late in the election season. A group called Mothers of the Movement, made up of families whose loved ones had been killed by police, endorsed Clinton as well. Samaria Rice, mother of twelve-year-old Tamir, wrote a letter in which she specifically did not endorse a candidate Kenrya Rankin, "Why Tamir Rice's Mom Hasn't Endorsed Anyone for President," *Colorlines,* March 15, 2016. So even that effort was not unanimous.

27. Joe Dinkin, "Bernie Sanders Blew a Huge Opportunity at Netroots Nation," *Nation,* July 22, 2015, www.thenation.com/article/bernie-sanders-blew-a-huge-opportunity-at-netroots-nation/.

28. Soon after this incident, Sanders hired the savvy Black communications director Symone Sanders and ramped up his appearances with prominent Black supporters like Cornel West, rapper Killer Mike, and Ben Jealous, but these efforts were not enough.

29. Jesse J. Holland, "AP Interview: Black Lives Matter Skipping 2016 Endorsement," *Associated Press,* September 19, 2015, https://apnews

.com/954d522f3299444ea5054e4bf451385e/ap-interview-black-lives-matter-skipping-2016-endorsement.

30. Black Futures Lab, "The Black Census Project," https://blackfutureslab.org/black-census-project/.

31. D.D. Guttenplan, "Is This the Most Radical Mayor in America?," *Nation,* November 17, 2017, www.thenation.com/article/is-this-the-most-radical-mayor-in-america/.

CHAPTER FIVE. THEMES, DILEMMAS, AND CHALLENGES

1. Beth Kowitt, "Why Mellody Hobson Stopped Apologizing for Being a Black Woman," *Fortune,* December 3, 2014, http://fortune.com/2014/12/03/mellody-hobson-next-gen/.

2. They don't necessarily use this term, although many do.

3. Peter Wallsten, "The Rev. Jeremiah Wright Was an Early Concern, Obama Aide Admits," *Top of the Ticket* (blog), *Los Angeles Times,* March 16, 2008, http://latimesblogs.latimes.com/washington/2008/03/throughout-his.html.

4. Steven Gray, "How Jeremiah Wright Found Religion," *Time,* April 29, 2008.

5. Rev. Jeremiah Wright, interview by Bill Moyers, *Bill Moyers Journal,* PBS, April 25, 2008, www.pbs.org/moyers/journal/04252008/watch.html.

6. Jay Caspian Kang, "'Our Demand Is Simple: Stop Killing Us,'" *New York Times Magazine,* May 4, 2015.

7. Jenna Wortham, "Black Tweets Matter," *Smithsonian Magazine,* September 2016, www.smithsonianmag.com/arts-culture/black-tweets-matter-180960117/.

8. Along with activist Brittany Packnett and technology strategist Sam Sinyangwe, Mckesson helped to produce a very polished website for a project dubbed "Campaign Zero" to advocate for police reform. The website features impressive and substantial research data and policy proposals in ten different areas and has broadened its scope since its inception.

9. Kang, "'Our Demand Is Simple.'"

10. See Michael Z. Muhammad, "Black Radical Conference Connects Youth with Elders and the Struggle," *Final Call,* January 21, 2016, www.finalcall.com/artman/publish/National_News_2/article_102860 .shtml.

11. Umi Selah, "Up You Mighty Race. Accomplish What You Will. What a Time. To Be Alive! What a Time. To Be Alive!" *Black Commentator* 637 (January 21, 2016), www.blackcommentator.com/637/637_up_ you_mighty_race_selah_guest.html.

12. Alisha Sonnier, interview with the author, St. Louis, Missouri, March 12, 2016.

13. Charlene Carruthers, "Not Your Grandfather's Black Freedom Movement: An Interview with BYP100's Charlene Carruthers," by Salim Muwakkil, *In These Times,* February 8, 2016, http://inthesetimes.com /article/18755/charlene-carruthers-on-byp200-Laquan-McDonald-and-police-violence.

14. Jonathan Lykes and Fresco Steez, "The Black Joy Experience Resource Guide," BYP100, 2017, 71.

15. Lamont Lilly, "Ferguson Activist Ashley Yates Talks Oakland, Assata Shakur and Black Woman Leadership," *Workers World,* July 20, 2017, www.workers.org/2017/07/20/ferguson-activist-ashley-yates-talks-oakland-assata-shakur-and-black-woman-leadership/.

16. Charlene Carruthers (February 15, 2017), Alicia Garza (March 9, 2017), Patrisse Khan-Cullors (April 11, 2017), and others, interviews with the author.

17. "About," Dream Defenders, www.dreamdefenders.org/about; "About BYP100," BYP100, https://byp100.org/about-byp100/#mission; "About," Black Lives Matter Global Network, https://blacklivesmatter .com/about/; Movement for Black Lives, "A Vision for Black Lives: Policy Demands for Black Power, Freedom and Justice," August 2016, https:// policy.m4bl.org/wp-content/uploads/2016/07/20160726-m4bl-Vision-Booklet-V3.pdf.

18. Andrea J. Ritchie, *Invisible No More: Police Violence against Black Women and Women of Color* (Boston: Beacon Press, 2017).

19. Rachel Gilmer, email interview with the author, August 14, 2017.

20. Sarah Larimer, "Disgraced Ex-cop Daniel Holtzclaw Sentenced to 263 Years for On-Duty Rapes, Sexual Assaults," *Washington*

Post, January 22, 2016, www.washingtonpost.com/news/post-nation/wp/2016/01/21/disgraced-ex-officer-daniel-holtzclaw-to-be-sentenced-after-sex-crimes-conviction/.

21. Steven W. Thrasher, "'No Indictment' for Sandra Bland: Black Women's Lives Just Don't Matter," *Guardian,* December 22, 2015, www.theguardian.com/commentisfree/2015/dec/22/no-indictment-for-sandra-bland-black-womens-lives-just-dont-matter.

22. Jamala Rogers, "#Cutthecheck Is Not a Movement," *St. Louis American,* May 28, 2015, www.stlamerican.com/ferguson/cutthecheck-is-not-a-movement/article_b712cdc0-04e4-11e5-824b-83e71b951fc3.html.

23. Darryl Holliday, "The New Black Power," *Chicago Magazine,* February 22, 2016, www.chicagomag.com/Chicago-Magazine/March-2016/black-leaders.

24. Aimee Levitt, "Black Youth Project 100 Suspends a Chicago Leader after Sexual Assault Allegation," *Chicago Reader,* December 3, 2015, www.chicagoreader.com/chicago/black-youth-project-100-suspends-leader-sexual-assault/Content?oid=20330409.

25. *NO! The Rape Documentary,* directed by Aishah Shahidah Simmons (Philadelphia: AfroLez Productions, 2006); Danielle McGuire, *At the Dark End of the Street: Black Women, Rape, and Resistance—A New History of the Civil Rights Movement from Rosa Parks to the Rise of Black Power* (New York: Alfred A. Knopf, 2010). For recent incidents of sexual harassment, see Caitlin Dickerson and Stephanie Saul, "Two Colleges Bound by History Are Roiled by the #MeToo Moment," *New York Times,* December 2, 2017, www.nytimes.com/2017/12/02/us/colleges-sexual-harassment.html.

26. For more information, see Harriet's Apothecary, www.harrietsapothecary.com.

27. "A Labor of Love: Black Mama's Bail Out Action + Reflection," Southerners on New Ground, May 16, 2017, http://southernersonnewground.org/2017/05/a-labor-of-love/.

28. The epigraph is from Charlene Carruthers, *Unapologetic: A Black, Queer and Feminist Mandate for Our Movement* (Boston: Beacon Press, forthcoming).

29. Numerous spectrogram exercises at meetings and retreats reveal that most participants are anticapitalist, although participants

may have different conceptions of what that stance actually means in practical terms.

30. Movement for Black Lives, "Vision for Black Lives."

31. BYP100, "Agenda to Build Black Futures," http://agendatobuild blackfutures.org/wp-content/uploads/2016/01/BYP_AgendaBlack Futures_booklet_web.pdf.

32. Between 2013 and 2017, after her partnership with fellow activist Janaya Khan, Patrisse Cullors changed her name to Patrisse Khan-Cullors.

33. Patrisse Khan-Cullors, phone interview with the author, April 11, 2017. See also Patrisse Khan-Cullors and asha bandele, *When They Call You a Terrorist: A Black Lives Matter Memoir* (New York: St. Martin's Press, 2018).

34. Rogers, "#Cutthecheck."

CHAPTER SIX. BACKLASH AND A PRICE

1. For example, see Jacquielynn Floyd, "This Is Dallas, This Is Our City, and We Don't Let Terrorism Win," *Dallas News*, July 8, 2016, www.dallasnews.com/opinion/commentary/2016/07/08/city-let-terrorism-win.

2. First Universalist Church of Minneapolis, "Press Release from the Group Black Lives Matter Minneapolis, Featuring a Statement from Rev. Justin Schroeder," Facebook, December 20, 2014, www.facebook.com/FirstUniv/posts/966243683405223.

3. Tribune News Services, "Jury Convicts Man Who Wounded Black Lives Matter Protesters in Minnesota," *Chicago Tribune*, February 1, 2017, www.chicagotribune.com/news/nationworld/ct-black-lives-matter-protesters-shooting-verdict-20170201-story.html.

4. Dani McClain, "The Bitter 'Black Lives Matter' Fight You Should Know About," *Talking Points Memo*, March 13, 2015, https://talkingpointsmemo.com/theslice/black-friday-14-oakland.

5. Kale Williams, "Alameda County D.A. Drops Charges against Black Friday 14," *SFGATE*, December 4, 2015, www.sfgate.com/bayarea/article/Alameda-County-DA-drops-against-Black-Friday-6675940.php.

6. Denise Hollinshed, "Ferguson Protester Who Set Fire at Berkeley QuikTrip Sentenced to 8 Years in Prison," *St. Louis Post-Dispatch*, December 10, 2015, www.stltoday.com/news/local/crime-and-courts/ferguson-protester-who-set-fire-at-berkeley-quiktrip-sentenced-to/article_aaed574c-3fb2-5f61-b599-7feef5a84cof.html.

7. Elizabeth Vega and Nabeegah Azeri, interview with the author, St. Louis, Missouri, March 12, 2016.

8. The title of the California state law has since been altered.

9. Melina Abdullah and Nana Gyamfi, "Black Lives Matter Activist Convicted of 'Felony Lynching': 'It's More Than Ironic, It's Disgusting,'" in conversation with Amy Goodman and Nermeen Shaikh, aired June 2, 2016, on *Democracy Now!*, www.democracynow.org/2016/6/2/black_lives_matter_activist_convicted_of.

10. Rosa A. Clemente (@rosaclemente), "Jasmine Richards, in Effect, Is the First Political Prisoner of the Black Lives Matter Movement. Everything …," Twitter, June 2, 2016, 11:50 p.m., https://twitter.com/rosaclemente/status/738623910996938752.

11. @Lester_Macgurdy, Twitter, June 3, 2016, 1:00 a.m. User account taken down.

12. In 1989, Trump took out a full-page newspaper ad condemning and castigating a group of Black teens wrongfully accused of the brutal rape and beating of a young white jogger in New York's Central Park. See Oliver Laughland, "Donald Trump and the Central Park Five: The Racially Charged Rise of a Demagogue," *Guardian*, February 17, 2016, www.theguardian.com/us-news/2016/feb/17/central-park-five-donald-trump-jogger-rape-case-new-york.

13. Carol Anderson, *White Rage: The Unspoken Truth of Our Racial Divide* (New York: Bloomsbury, 2016).

14. See Carol Robinson, "Black Protester Attacked at Donald Trump Rally Called 'Monkey' and Other Racial Slurs, He Claims," *AL.com*, updated October 18, 2016, www.al.com/news/birmingham/index.ssf/2015/11/black_protester_attacked_at_do.html; Rachel Dicker, "Man at Trump Rally Yells 'Go Back to Africa' at Black Woman," *U.S. News and World Report*, March 14, 2016, https://www.usnews.com/news/articles/2016-03-14/man-at-trump-rally-yells-go-back-to-africa-at-black-woman.

15. See Jennifer Calfas, "Trump Supporter Apologizes to Protester for Punching Him," *The Hill*, December 14, 2016, http://thehill.com /blogs/blog-briefing-room/news/310484-trump-supporter-who-sucker-punched-protester-apologizes; Lizzie Dearden, "Donald Trump Supporters Push and Shove Young Black Woman as Protesters Thrown Out of Kentucky Rally," *Independent*, March 2, 2016, www.independent .co.uk/news/world/americas/donald-trump-supporters-push-young-black-woman-protesters-thrown-out-of-kentucky-louisville-rally-a6906836.html.

16. Tyler Cherry, "How Fox News' Primetime Lineup Demonized Black Lives Matter in 2015," *Media Matters for America* (blog), December 29, 2015, http://mediamatters.org/blog/2015/12/29/how-fox-news-primetime-lineup-demonized-black-l/207637; Hilary Hanson and Simon McCormack, "Fox News Suggests Black Lives Matter Is a 'Murder' Movement, 'Hate Group,'" *Huffington Post*, September 1, 2015, www.huffingtonpost .com/entry/black-lives-matter-fox-news-hate-group_us_55e5c102e4 b0b7a9633a3b12.

17. Jana Winter and Sharon Weinberger, "The FBI's New U.S. Terrorist Threat: 'Black Identity Extremists,'" *Foreign Policy*, October 6, 2017, http://foreignpolicy.com/2017/10/06/the-fbi-has-identified-a-new-domestic-terrorist-threat-and-its-black-identity-extremists/.

18. Michael E. Miller, "Black Lives Matter Activist Kills Himself on Steps of Ohio Statehouse," *Washington Post*, February 9, 2016, www .washingtonpost.com/news/morning-mix/wp/2016/02/09/black-lives-matter-activist-kills-himself-on-steps-of-ohio-statehouse/; Wesley Lowery and Kevin Stankiewicz, "'My Demons Won Today': Ohio Activist's Suicide Spotlights Depression among Black Lives Matter Leaders," *Washington Post*, February 15, 2016, www.washingtonpost.com/news /post-nation/wp/2016/02/15/my-demons-won-today-ohio-activists-suicide-spotlights-depression-among-black-lives-matter-leaders/.

19. Opal Tometi, email interview with the author, November 27, 2017.

20. Assata Shakur, *Assata: An Autobiography* (Lawrence Hill Books, 1987).

CHAPTER SEVEN. A VIEW FROM THE LOCAL

1. "Do Black Lives Matter? Robin DG Kelley and Fred Moten in Conversation," *Critical Resistance*, aired January 8, 2015, on Vimeo, 1:25:36, https://vimeo.com/116111740.

2. For further information, see Jeffrey Hass, *The Assassination of Fred Hampton: How the FBI and the Chicago Police Murdered a Black Panther* (Chicago: Lawrence Hill Books, 2010); Joshua Bloom and Waldo E. Martin Jr., *Black against Empire: The History and Politics of the Black Panther Party* (Oakland: University of California Press, 2016).

3. Ken Armstrong and Steve Mills, "Ryan Suspends Death Penalty," *Chicago Tribune*, January 31, 2000.

4. Alice Kim, email interview with the author, December 26, 2017.

5. See Chicago Public Schools, *Reparations Won: A Case Study in Police Torture, Racism, and the Movement for Justice in Chicago* (Chicago: Department of Social Science and Civic Engagement, 2017), https://blog.cps.edu/wp-content/uploads/2017/08/ReparationsWon_HighSchool.pdf.

6. Adam Sege, "Man Dies after Chicago Police Use Taser during Arrest," *Chicago Tribune*, May 21, 2014, www.chicagotribune.com/news/local/breaking/chi-man-tased-by-police-while-resisting-arrest-dies-20140521-story.html.

7. The 1951 "We Charge Genocide: The Crime of Government against the Negro People" document and petition chronicled instances of lynching and sought to put the issue on an international agenda. It was spearheaded by the left-wing Civil Rights Congress, and petitions were submitted to UN representatives in New York and Paris. For more details about the 1951 petition, see Charles H. Martin, "Internationalizing 'The American Dilemma': The Civil Rights Congress and the 1951 Genocide," *Journal of American Ethnic History* 16, no. 4 (1997): 35–61.

8. Heather Cherone, "Police Misconduct Cases Cost City Taxpayers $10.2 Million (Just This Week)," *DNAinfo*, updated September 8, 2017, www.dnainfo.com/chicago/20170906/jackson-highlands/102-million-city-money-goes-settle-4-police-misconduct-cases.

9. Jasson Perez, email interview with the author, November 4, 2017.

10. Akiba Solomon, "Chicago Woman Groped by Cop Found Innocent of Eavesdropping," *Colorlines,* August 29, 2011, www.colorlines.com /articles/chicago-woman-groped-cop-found-innocent-eavesdropping.

11. Mariame Kaba, "Four Years since a Chicago Police Officer Killed Rekia Boyd, Justice Still Hasn't Been Served," *In These Times,* March 21, 2016, http://inthesetimes.com/article/18989/four-years-since-the-shooting-of-rekia-boyd.

12. Kim Bellware, "Chicago Cop Who Killed Rekia Boyd Quits, Preserving His Cushy Retirement," *Huffington Post,* May 17, 2016, www.huffingtonpost.com/entry/dante-servin-quits_us_573b7f22e4b0ef 86171c6575.

13. "#FireDanteServin: An Abolitionist Campaign in Chicago," *Prison Culture* (blog), September 19, 2015, www.usprisonculture.com /blog/2015/09/19/firedanteservin-an-abolitionist-campaign-in-chicago/.

14. Mariame Kaba, email interview with the author, October 23, 2017.

15. Darryl Holliday, "The New Black Power," *Chicago Magazine,* February 22, 2016, www.chicagomag.com/Chicago-Magazine/March-2016/ black-leaders/; Monica Davey and Mitch Smith, "Chicago Police Dept. Plagued by Systemic Racism, Task Force Finds," *New York Times,* April 13, 2016, www.nytimes.com/2016/04/14/us/chicago-police-dept-plagued-by-systemic-racism-task-force-finds.html.

16. Ted Cox, "Fire Dante Servin, Demand Protesters, Who Also Want Chicago State Funded," *DNAinfo,* April 20, 2016, www.dnainfo .com/chicago/20160420/downtown/fire-dante-servin-protest-set-for-wednesday-afternoon-outside-rahms-office.

17. Kelly Hayes, "Black Organizers in Chicago Get in 'Formation' for Black Lives and Public Education," *Truthout,* May 10, 2016, www .truth-out.org/news/item/35962-inspired-by-beyonce-black-organizers-get-in-formation-to-disrupt-nfl-draft.

18. Derrick Clifton, "Queer Women Are Shaping Chicago's Black Lives Matter Movement," *Chicago Reader,* April 7, 2016, www .chicagoreader.com/chicago/queer-black-women-shaping-black-lives-matter/Content?oid=21692933.

19. Jennifer Chukwu, "A Visible Love, A Visible Movement: An Interview with Veronica Morris-Moore," Black Youth Project, March 15, 2016, http://blackyouthproject.com/a-visible-love-a-visible-movement-interview-with-veronica-morris-moore/.

20. See Brandon Smith, "Why I'm Suing the Chicago Police Department," *Chicago Reader*, August 7, 2015, www.chicagoreader.com/Bleader /archives/2015/08/07/why-im-suing-the-chicago-police-department; Julie Bosman, "Journalist Who Told Laquan McDonald's Story Faces Fight over Sources," *New York Times*, updated December 13, 2017, www .nytimes.com/2017/11/26/us/chicago-police-shooting-journalist-laquan-mcdonald.html; Craig Futterman and Jamie Kalven, "Laquan McDonald," Invisible Institute, December 8, 2014, https://invisible.institute /news/2014/laquan-mcdonald.

21. Steve Schmadeke, "Judge Who Has Heard High-Profile Cases Could Decide Officer Van Dyke's Fate," *Chicago Tribune*, December 29, 2015, www.chicagotribune.com/news/local/breaking/ct-jason-van-dyke-laquan-mcdonald-arraignment-20151229-story.html.

22. Leah Hope and Laura Thoren, "Kim Foxx Defeats Anita Alvarez in Cook County State's Attorney Primary," aired March 16, 2016, on ABC 7 Chicago, http://abc7chicago.com/politics/foxx-defeats-alvarez-in-cook-county-states-attorney-primary/1247992/.

23. "An Introduction to Mijente," Mijente, December 10, 2015, https://mijente.net/2015/12/10/an-introduction-to-mijente/.

24. Marisa Franco, "A Radical Expansion of Sanctuary: Steps in Defiance of Trump's Executive Order," *Truthout*, January 25, 2017, www.truth-out.org/opinion/item/39224-a-radical-expansion-of-sanctuary-steps-in-defiance-of-trump-s-executive-order.

CHAPTER EIGHT. POLITICAL QUILTERS AND MAROON SPACES

1. Denise Perry, interview with the author, Franklinton, North Carolina, February 24, 2017.

2. Perry, interview.

3. Thenjiwe McHarris, phone interview with the author, October 26, 2017.

4. McHarris, interview.

5. Maurice (Moe) Mitchell, phone interview with the author, October 26, 2017.

6. Robin D. G. Kelley, "What Does Black Lives Matter Want?," *Boston Review*, August 17, 2016.

7. Chinyere Tutashinda, email interview with the author, January 8, 2018.

CONCLUSION

The epigraph is from Derrick Clifton, "Queer Women Are Shaping Chicago's Black Lives Matter Movement," *Chicago Reader,* April 7, 2016, www.chicagoreader.com/chicago/queer-black-women-shaping-black-lives-matter/Content?oid=21692933.

1. Ruth Wilson Gilmore and Craig Gilmore, "Beyond Bratton," in *Policing the Planet: Why the Policing Crisis Led to Black Lives Matter,* eds. Jordan T. Camp and Christina Heatherton (New York: Verso, 2016), 197.

2. Gilmore and Gilmore, "Beyond Bratton," 198.

3. Gus Speth, "System Change and Non-Reformist Reforms," *Truthout,* October 15, 2015, www.truth-out.org/speakout/item/33255-system-change-and-non-reformist-reforms.

4. Keeanga-Yamahtta Taylor, *From #BlackLivesMatter to Black Liberation* (Chicago: Haymarket Books, 2016), 219.

5. Shawn Gude, "Why Baltimore Rebelled," *Jacobin,* April 28, 2015, www.jacobinmag.com/2015/04/baltimore-freddie-gray-unrest-protests.

6. Gwen Carr, "Mother of Eric Garner: Racial and Economic Justice Go Hand-in-Hand," *New York Daily News,* November 10, 2015, www.nydailynews.com/new-york/eric-garner-mom-racial-economic-justice-hand-in-hand-article-1.2428874.

7. Combahee River Collective, "The Combahee River Collective Statement," April 1977, http://circuitous.org/scraps/combahee.html.

8. "From the Kennedy Commission to the Combahee Collective: Black Feminist Organizing, 1960–80," by Duchess Harris in *Sisters in*

Struggle: African American Women in the Civil Rights Movement, Bettye Collier-Thomas and V. P. Franklin, eds. (New York University Press, 2001), 297.

9. Jeffrey D. Sachs, "The GOP Tax Cut Is Daylight Robbery," *Boston Globe,* November 14, 2017, www.bostonglobe.com/opinion/2017/11/13/the-gop-tax-cut-daylight-robbery/0FF1Y8MFy7rH8eyEzWA7iM/story.html.

10. Homi Bhabha, *The Location of Culture* (1994; repr., New York: Routledge, 2012), 59.

GLOSSARY

ABOLITION Derives from the contemporary prison abolition movement and borrows from the nineteenth-century movement to
abolish chattel slavery. It refers to the goal of eliminating the need
for prisons by addressing the social and economic bases for behav-
iors deemed criminal and finding alternatives to incarceration
formed on the basis of a restorative justice model that focuses on
making amends, healing, and restitution. Ruth Wilson Gilmore,
Angela Davis, and the organization Critical Resistance have been
important catalysts in this movement.

BLACKBIRD Founded in the wake of the 2014 Ferguson uprising by
Thenjiwe McHarris, Merv Marcano, and Maurice Mitchell, this is
a strategy and communications team that has been instrumental in
the emergence of the Movement for Black Lives.

BLACK LIVES MATTER GLOBAL NETWORK (BLMGN) Formed in 2014 as
an outgrowth of the #BlackLivesMatter social media campaign to
oppose anti-Black racism and state violence.

BLACK YOUTH PROJECT 100 (BYP100) National organization of eighteen-
to thirty-five-year-old Black organizers founded in 2013 and committed to organizing for Black liberation through "a Black queer
feminist lens."

CROSS-MOVEMENT ORGANIZING Organizing or collaborations that link and involve not simply multiple organizations but multiple networks of organizations, such as the Movement for Black Lives and the environmental justice movement.

DREAM DEFENDERS Statewide Florida-based activist organization led by young people of color and founded in 2012 in response to Trayvon Martin's murder.

HETERO-PATRIARCHY The structural and institutional practices and values that reinscribe male power, authority, and centrality in communities, in families, and in the dominant political, economic, and cultural institutions of a society. The normalization and privileging of heterosexual practices and relationships work in tandem with the assumption that men should be the "heads" of families and the leaders of communities, organizations, and society.

INTERSECTIONALITY Coined by critical-race-theory scholar Kimberlé Crenshaw in 1989, *intersectionality* refers to interlocking and mutually reinforcing systems of oppression and inseparable categories of identity, most notably race, class, gender, and sexuality. This analytical and political approach preceded Crenshaw's naming of it and is reflected in the work of Black feminist scholars and activists, including Audre Lorde, Angela Davis, bell hooks, Barbara Smith, and Beverly Guy-Sheftall, and in the Combahee River Collective statement of 1977, considered a foundational Black feminist manifesto.

MILLION HOODIES MOVEMENT FOR JUSTICE A New York–based activist organization led by Dante Berry. It was sparked by protests after Trayvon Martin's murder but has expanded to address a range of human rights issues.

MOVEMENT FOR BLACK LIVES (M4BL) An umbrella coalition that includes most of the major organizations associated with the Black Lives Matter Movement.

NEOLIBERALISM First advanced in the nineteenth century, it currently refers to privatization, deregulation, and a kind of laissez-faire capitalism, according to which the government plays a minimal role and the free market supposedly governs the econ-

omy. Milton Friedman is closely associated with neoliberal
policies, such as those he advised the Pinochet government to
implement in Chile after the US-backed coup that ousted the
democratically elected president Salvador Allende. David Harvey,
Marxist geographer and critic of neoliberalism, views it as the
capitalist instrumentalization of politics. In a neoliberal frame, the
market is supreme.

PRAXIS The merging of theory and practice.

RACIAL CAPITALISM Refers to the inextricable connections between
white supremacy and modern capitalism, as exemplified by the
transatlantic slave trade and race-based slavery in the Americas,
colonialism and imperialism, and various forms of forced racial
segregation that reinforce economic subordination and exploitation. It is a concept informed by the work of Cedric Robinson in
his foundational book *Black Marxism,* which is both a leftist and
radical historical analysis and a critique of orthodox Marxist
views of race.

SAY HER NAME The title of a report—issued by the African American
Policy Forum and then embraced by Black Lives Matter Movement organizations, led by BYP100—which has been a catalyst for
demonstrations and vigils that draw attention to women and
femmes who have been victims of police violence.

STATE VIOLENCE Different theorists and activists might use this term
differently, but for the purposes of this book, it refers not only to
police violence but to the policies that enact physical and psychological harm and are either endorsed or administered by the state
(government).

KEY FIGURES

REKIA BOYD Twenty-two-year-old Black woman, whose death was a catalyst for protests against police violence after she was killed by an off-duty Chicago police officer in 2012.

MICHAEL BROWN Victim of a fatal August 2014 police shooting in Ferguson, Missouri, that resulted in a massive uprising in the town, which had national repercussions and was seen as the spark for the Black Lives Matter Movement.

CHARLENE CARRUTHERS Chicago native, organizer, author, and founding director of BYP100.

CATHY COHEN Political scientist and scholar-activist—the impetus for, and an early supporter of, BYP100, who played an instrumental role in its founding.

BRITTANY FERRELL St. Louis resident, who became a leader of the 2014 Ferguson protests in the wake of the police killing of Michael Brown.

KORRYN GAINES Black mother of two, who was killed by police in her home outside Baltimore, which resulted in more anti–police violence protests.

ALICIA GARZA One of three cofounders of #BlackLivesMatter and the Black Lives Matter Global Network, Oakland-based activist and a director of the National Domestic Workers Alliance.

FREDDIE GRAY Twenty-five-year-old Baltimore resident whose death in police custody in 2015 sparked massive protests in the city.

PATRISSE KHAN-CULLORS Organizer, author, and California-based cofounder of #BlackLivesMatter and the Black Lives Matter Global Network.

TRAYVON MARTIN Seventeen-year-old Black boy, who was killed by local, volunteer neighborhood watchman George Zimmerman in Sanford, Florida, in 2012, in a case of racial profiling that sparked protests nationwide.

TEF POE Poet, musician, rapper, and activist from St. Louis, who was part of the Ferguson protests after Michael Brown's murder.

OPAL TOMETI One of the three cofounders of #BlackLivesMatter and the director of the Black Alliance for Just Immigration and the national Freedom Cities campaign.

SELECTED BIBLIOGRAPHY

In addition to published books, articles, interviews, and reports, the author relied on thousands of tweets, blog posts, Facebook posts, and online news sources, which constitute the twenty-first-century archive for this movement. The following list is not exhaustive. As a participant-observer in the movement, the author has also collected thousands of pages of personal notes, flyers, agendas, minutes, and memos, which are rich primary sources.

BOOKS

Alexander, Michelle. *The New Jim Crow: Mass Incarceration in the Age of Colorblindness*. New York: New Press, 2010.

Anderson, Carol. *White Rage: The Unspoken Truth of Our Racial Divide*. New York: Bloomsbury, 2016.

Bhabha, Homi. *The Location of Culture*. New York: Routledge, 2012. First published 1994.

Bloom, Joshua, and Waldo E. Martin Jr. *Black against Empire: The History and Politics of the Black Panther Party*. Oakland: University of California Press, 2016.

Camp, Jordan T., and Christina Heatherton, eds. *Policing the Planet: Why the Policing Crisis Led to Black Lives Matter*. New York: Verso, 2016.

Carruthers, Charlene. *Unapologetic: A Black, Queer and Feminist Mandate for Our Movement*. Boston: Beacon Press, forthcoming.

Coates, Ta-Nehisi. *Between the World and Me*. New York: Spiegel and Grau, 2015.

Cohen, Cathy J. *Democracy Remixed: Black Youth and the Future of American Politics*. New York: Oxford University Press, 2010.

Davis, Angela Y. *Freedom Is a Constant Struggle: Ferguson, Palestine, and the Foundations of a Movement*. Chicago: Haymarket Books, 2016.

————. *Women, Race, and Class*. New York: Random House, 1981.

Dyson, Michael Eric. *The Black Presidency: Barack Obama and the Politics of Race in America*. New York: Houghton Mifflin Harcourt, 2016.

Forman, James, Jr. *Locking Up Our Own: Crime and Punishment in Black America*. New York: Farrar, Straus and Giroux, 2017.

Gilmore, Ruth Wilson. *Golden Gulag: Prisons, Surplus, Crisis, and Opposition in Globalizing California*. Berkeley: University of California Press, 2007.

Glaude, Eddie S., Jr. *Democracy in Black: How Race Still Enslaves the American Soul*. New York: Broadway Books, 2016.

Guy-Sheftall, Beverly, ed. *Words of Fire: An Anthology of African-American Feminist Thought*. New York: New Press, 1995.

Harcourt, Bernard E. *Illusion of Order: The False Promise of Broken Windows Policing*. Cambridge, MA: Harvard University Press, 2001.

Harris, Frederick C. *The Price of the Ticket: Barack Obama and the Rise and Decline of Black Politics*. New York: Oxford University Press, 2012.

Hass, Jeffrey. *The Assassination of Fred Hampton: How the FBI and the Chicago Police Murdered a Black Panther*. Chicago: Lawrence Hill Books, 2010.

Hill, Marc Lamont. *Nobody: Casualties of America's War on the Vulnerable, from Ferguson to Flint and Beyond*. New York: Atria Books, 2016.

hooks, bell. *Feminist Theory: From Margin to Center*. Cambridge, MA: South End Press, 1984.

Khan-Cullors, Patrisse, and asha bandele. *When They Call You a Terrorist: A Black Lives Matter Memoir*. New York: St. Martin's Press, 2018.

Lang, Clarence. *Grassroots at the Gateway: Class Politics and Black Freedom Struggle in St. Louis, 1936–75*. Ann Arbor: University of Michigan Press, 2009.

LeBron, Christopher. *The Making of Black Lives Matter: The Brief History of an Idea.* New York: Oxford University Press, 2017.

Lowery, Wesley. *They Can't Kill Us All: Ferguson, Baltimore and a New Era in America's Racial Justice Movement.* New York: Little, Brown, 2016.

McSpadden, Lezley. *Tell the Truth & Shame the Devil: The Life, Legacy and Love of My Son Michael Brown.* New York: Regan Arts, 2016.

Morris, Aldon D. *The Origins of the Civil Rights Movement: Black Communities Organizing for Change.* New York: Free Press, 1984.

Richie, Beth E. *Arrested Justice: Black Women, Violence, and America's Prison Nation.* New York: New York University Press, 2012.

Ritchie, Andrea J. *Invisible No More: Police Violence against Black Women and Women of Color.* Boston: Beacon Press, 2017.

Robinson, Cedric. *Black Marxism: The Making of the Black Radical Tradition.* Chapel Hill: University of North Carolina Press, 2000. First published 1983 by Zed Press (London).

Rogers, Jamala. *Ferguson Is America: Roots of Rebellion.* Mira Digital, 2015.

Smiley, Tavis, ed. *The Covenant with Black America—Ten Years Later.* Carlsbad, CA: Smiley Books, 2016.

Smith, Mychal Denzel. *Invisible Man, Got the Whole World Watching: A Young Black Man's Education.* New York: Nation Books, 2016.

Taylor, Keeanga-Yamahtta. *From #BlackLivesMatter to Black Liberation.* Chicago: Haymarket Books, 2016.

ARTICLES, PERIODICALS, AND REPORTS

Ackerman, Spencer. "US Police Given Billions from Homeland Security for 'Tactical' Equipment." *Guardian,* August 20, 2014. www .theguardian.com/world/2014/aug/20/police-billions-homeland-security-military-equipment.

Alexander, Michelle. "Why Hillary Clinton Doesn't Deserve the Black Vote." *Nation,* February 10, 2016.

Anderson, Jessica, and Christiana Amarachi Mbakwe. "Korryn Gaines Was Passionate about Beliefs, Anticipated Violent Confrontation with Police." *Baltimore Sun,* August 5, 2016. www.baltimoresun.com /news/maryland/crime/bs-md-co-korryn-gaines-profile-20160804-story.html.

Apuzzo, Matt. "Ferguson Police Routinely Violate Rights of Blacks, Justice Dept. Finds." *New York Times,* March 3, 2015.

Armstrong, Ken, and Steve Mills. "Ryan Suspends Death Penalty." *Chicago Tribune,* January 31, 2000.

Associated Press. "Trayvon Martin Death: Thousands March in Town Where Teenager Was Shot." *Guardian,* March 31, 2012. www .theguardian.com/world/2012/mar/31/trayvon-martin-protest-march-sanford.

Bailey, Kristian Davis. "Dream Defenders, Black Lives Matter & Ferguson Reps Take Historic Trip to Palestine." *Ebony,* January 9, 2015.

Bellware, Kim. "Chicago Cop Who Killed Rekia Boyd Quits, Preserving His Cushy Retirement." *Huffington Post,* May 17, 2016. www.huffington post.com/entry/dante-servin-quits_us_573b7f22e4b0ef86171c6575.

Berlatsky, Noah. "The Women of #BlackLivesMatter." *Atlantic,* January 27, 2015. www.theatlantic.com/national/archive/2015/01/women-and-blacklivesmatter/384855/.

Binelli, Mark. "The Fire Last Time." *New Republic,* April 6, 2017. https:// newrepublic.com/article/141701/fire-last-time-detroit-stress-police-squad-terrorized-black-community.

Black Scholar. "The Black Radical Congress: A Black Freedom Agenda for the Twenty-First Century." Vol. 28, no. 1 (1998): 71–73.

Black Youth Project 100. "Agenda to Build Black Futures." http:// agendatobuildblackfutures.org/wp-content/uploads/2016/01/BYP_AgendaBlackFutures_booklet_web.pdf.

Brydum, Sunnivie. "Watch: 'We Don't Want Reform, We Want Revolution.'" *Advocate,* February 7, 2015. www.advocate.com/politics /2015/02/07/watch-we-dont-want-reform-we-want-revolution.

Caldwell, Erica. "Where My Girls At: Meet Two of Ferguson's Black Queer Activists." *Bitch Media,* April 27, 2015. www.bitchmedia.org /post/where-my-girls-at-meet-fergusons-black-queer-activists.

Capehart, Jonathan. "Marilyn Mosby's Amazing Press Conference." *Washington Post,* May 1, 2015. www.washingtonpost.com/blogs/post-partisan/wp/2015/05/01/marilyn-mosbys-amazing-press-conference/.

Carr, Gwen. "Mother of Eric Garner: Racial and Economic Justice Go Hand-in-Hand." *New York Daily News,* November 10, 2015. www

.nydailynews.com/new-york/eric-garner-mom-racial-economic-justice-hand-in-hand-article-1.2428874.

Carruthers, Charlene. "Black Power: A Q & A with Charlene Carruthers." *Black Youth Project*, February 11, 2016. http://blackyouthproject.com /black-power-a-qa-with-charlene-carruthers/.

———. "In Defense of Korryn Gaines, Black Women and Children." *Colorlines*, August 5, 2016. www.colorlines.com/articles/defense-korryn-gaines-black-women-and-children-opinion.

———. "Not Your Grandfather's Black Freedom Movement: An Interview with BYP100's Charlene Carruthers." By Salim Muwakkil. *In These Times*, February 8, 2016. http://inthesetimes.com /article/18755/charlene-carruthers-on-byp200-Laquan-McDonald-and-police-violence.

Cherone, Heather. "Police Misconduct Cases Cost City Taxpayers $10.2 Million (Just This Week)." *DNAinfo*, updated September 8, 2017. www.dnainfo.com/chicago/20170906/jackson-highlands/102-million-city-money-goes-settle-4-police-misconduct-cases.

Cherry, Tyler. "How Fox News' Primetime Lineup Demonized Black Lives Matter in 2015." *Media Matters for America* (blog). December 29, 2015. http://mediamatters.org/blog/2015/12/29/how-fox-news-primetime-lineup-demonized-black-l/207637.

Chicago Public Schools. *Reparations Won: A Case Study in Police Torture, Racism, and the Movement for Justice in Chicago*. Chicago: Department of Social Science and Civic Engagement, 2017.

Clifton, Derrick. "Queer Women Are Shaping Chicago's Black Lives Matter Movement." *Chicago Reader*, April 7, 2016.

Cobb, Jelani. "The Matter of Black Lives." *New Yorker*, March 14, 2016.

Cohen, Debra Nussbaum. "The Jewish Activist behind the Black Lives Matter Platform Calling Israel's Treatment of Palestinians 'Genocide.'" *Haaretz*, August 10, 2016. www.haaretz.com/world-news /americas/.premium-1.735865.

Colón, Kristiana Rae. "Showdown at Beauty Town." *Lost Voices* (blog). October 1, 2014. www.thelostvoices.org/blog. Site discontinued.

Cooper, Brittney. "In Defense of Black Rage: Michael Brown, Police and the American Dream." *Salon*, August 12, 2014. www.salon

.com/2014/08/12/in_defense_of_black_rage_michael_brown_police_
and_the_american_dream/.

Crenshaw, Kimberlé. "Demarginalizing the Intersection of Race and
Sex: A Black Feminist Critique of Antidiscrimination Doctrine,
Feminist Theory and Antiracist Politics." *University of Chicago Legal
Forum* 1 (1989): 139–67.

Crenshaw, Kimberlé, and Andrea J. Ritchie. *Say Her Name: Resisting
Police Brutality against Black Women.* African American Policy Forum.
Center for Intersectionality and Social Policy Studies. New York:
Columbia University Law School, May 2015 (updated July 2015).

Davis, Angela Y. "Masked Racism: Reflections on the Prison Industrial Complex." *Colorlines,* September 10, 1998. www.colorlines.com
/articles/masked-racism-reflections-prison-industrial-complex.

Devereaux, Ryan. "Echoes of Trayvon Martin as Residents Seek Justice for Bronx Teen's Death." *Guardian,* March 30, 2012. www
.theguardian.com/world/2012/mar/30/trayvon-martin-ramarley-graham-
bronx-teenager.

Dicker, Rachel. "Man at Trump Rally Yells 'Go Back to Africa' at
Black Woman." *U.S. News and World Report,* March 14, 2016. www.
usnews.com/news/articles/2016-03-14/man-at-trump-rally-yells-go-
back-to-africa-at-black-woman.

Dickerson, Caitlin, and Stephanie Saul. "Two Colleges Bound by
History Are Roiled by the #MeToo Moment." *New York Times,*
December 2, 2017. www.nytimes.com/2017/12/02/us/colleges-sexual-
harassment.html.

Elzie, Johnetta. "A Poem about the Women's March by Johnetta Elzie."
Teen Vogue, January 23, 2017. www.teenvogue.com/story/a-poem-by-
johnetta-elzie.

Fenton, Justin. "Freddie Gray Case: Judge Allows Malicious Prosecution
Lawsuit against Mosby to Proceed." *Baltimore Sun,* January 6, 2017.

———. "Independent Review Faults City Police in Tyrone West Case."
Baltimore Sun, August 8, 2014. http://articles.baltimoresun.com/2014-
08-08/news/bs-md-ci-tyrone-west-outside-review-20140808_1_tyrone-
west-james-chips-stewart-excessive-force.

———. "Tyrone West Files Show Passenger's Account of Death in
Police Custody." *Baltimore Sun,* January 23, 2014. http://articles

.baltimoresun.com/2014-01-23/news/bs-md-ci-tyrone-west-witness-20140122_1_tyrone-west-jorge-bernardez-ruiz-kitmore-road.

Fenwick, Ben, and Alan Schwarz. "In Rape Case of Oklahoma Officer, Victims Hope Convictions Will Aid Cause." *New York Times,* December 11, 2015.

Ferrell, Brittany, and Alexis Templeton. "[Ferguson Forward] Brittany and Alexis: In Love and Struggle." Interview by Jamilah Lemieux. *Ebony,* August 7, 2015. www.ebony.com/news-views/ferguson-forward-brittany-and-alexis-in-love-and-struggle-404.

Floyd, Jacquielynn. "This Is Dallas, This Is Our City, and We Don't Let Terrorism Win." *Dallas News,* July 8, 2016. www.dallasnews.com/opinion/commentary/2016/07/08/city-let-terrorism-win.

Franco, Marisa. "A Radical Expansion of Sanctuary: Steps in Defiance of Trump's Executive Order." *Truthout,* January 25, 2017. www.truth-out.org/opinion/item/39224-a-radical-expansion-of-sanctuary-steps-in-defiance-of-trump-s-executive-order.

Futterman, Craig, and Jamie Kalven. "Laquan McDonald." Invisible Institute, December 8, 2014. https://invisible.institute/news/2014/laquan-mcdonald.

Gray, Steven. "How Jeremiah Wright Found Religion." *Time,* April 29, 2008.

Gruberg, Sharita. "How For-Profit Companies Are Driving Immigration Detention Policies." *Center for American Progress,* December 18, 2015. www.americanprogress.org/issues/immigration/reports/2015/12/18/127769/how-for-profit-companies-are-driving-immigration-detention-policies/.

Gude, Shawn. "Why Baltimore Rebelled." *Jacobin,* April 28, 2015. www.jacobinmag.com/2015/04/baltimore-freddie-gray-unrest-protests.

Harris, Fredrick C. "The Rise of Respectability Politics." *Dissent,* Winter 2014.

Hayes, Kelly. "Black Organizers in Chicago Get in 'Formation' for Black Lives and Public Education." *Truthout,* May 10, 2016. www.truth-out.org/news/item/35962-inspired-by-beyonce-black-organizers-get-in-formation-to-disrupt-nfl-draft.

Holliday, Darryl. "The New Black Power." *Chicago Magazine,* February 22, 2016. www.chicagomag.com/Chicago-Magazine/March-2016/black-leaders.

Hollinshed, Denise. "Ferguson Protester Who Set Fire at Berkeley QuikTrip Sentenced to 8 Years in Prison." *St. Louis Post-Dispatch*, December 10, 2015. www.stltoday.com/news/local/crime-and-courts /ferguson-protester-who-set-fire-at-berkeley-quiktrip-sentenced-to /article_aaed574c-3fb2-5f61-b599-7feef5a84c0f.html.

Horowitz, Juliana Menasce, and Gretchen Livingston. "How Americans View the Black Lives Matter Movement." *FactTank* (blog). Pew Research Center, July 8, 2016. www.pewresearch.org/fact-tank/2016 /07/08/how-americans-view-the-black-lives-matter-movement/.

Hunt, Elle. "Alicia Garza on the Beauty and Burden of Black Lives Matter." *Guardian,* September 2, 2016.

Hylton, Wil S. "Baltimore vs. Marilyn Mosby." *New York Times Magazine,* September 28, 2016.

Jaffe, Sarah. "Young Activists Occupy Florida Capitol, Demand Justice for Trayvon." *In These Times,* July 25, 2013. http://inthesetimes.com /article/15356/young_activists_occupy_florida_capitol_demand_ justice_for_trayvon.

Kaba, Mariame. "Four Years since a Chicago Police Officer Killed Rekia Boyd, Justice Still Hasn't Been Served." *In These Times,* March 21, 2016. http://inthesetimes.com/article/18989/four-years- since-the-shooting-of-rekia-boyd.

Kelley, Robin D.G. "What Does Black Lives Matter Want?" *Boston Review,* August 17, 2016.

King, Jay Caspian. "'Our Demand Is Simple: Stop Killing Us.'" *New York Times Magazine,* May 4, 2015.

King, Martin Luther, Jr. "Beyond Vietnam." Speech given at the Riverside Church, New York, April 4, 1967. The Martin Luther King Jr. Research and Education Institute, Stanford University.

Korn, Gabrielle. "This Is What It's Like to Be a Youth Activist in Ferguson." *Nylon,* December 2, 2014. https://nylon.com/articles/brittany- ferrell-interview.

Lee, Trymaine. "Trayvon Martin Case Protests across Nation Culminate with Show of Strength in Florida." *Huffington Post,* March 23, 2012. www.huffingtonpost.com/2012/03/23/trayvon-martin-rally- national-protest_n_1375699.html.

Levitt, Aimee. "Black Youth Project 100 Suspends a Chicago Leader after Sexual Assault Allegation." *Chicago Reader,* December 3, 2015. www.chicagoreader.com/chicago/black-youth-project-100-suspends-leader-sexual-assault/Content?oid=20330409.

Lilly, Lamont. "Ferguson Activist Ashley Yates Talks Oakland, Assata Shakur and Black Woman Leadership." *Workers World,* July 20, 2017. www.workers.org/2017/07/20/ferguson-activist-ashley-yates-talks-oakland-assata-shakur-and-black-woman-leadership/.

Lowery, Wesley, and Kevin Stankiewicz. "'My Demons Won Today': Ohio Activist's Suicide Spotlights Depression among Black Lives Matter Leaders." *Washington Post,* February 15, 2016. www.washington post.com/news/post-nation/wp/2016/02/15/my-demons-won-today-ohio-activists-suicide-spotlights-depression-among-black-lives-matter-leaders.

Luscombe, Richard. "Jury Hears Emotional Opening Statements in George Zimmerman Trial." *Guardian,* June 24, 2013. www.theguardian.com/world/2013/jun/24/george-zimmerman-trial-opening-statements.

Marbella, Jean. "Beginning of Freddie Gray's Life as Sad as Its End, Court Case Shows." *Baltimore Sun,* April 23, 2015. www.baltimoresun.com/news/maryland/baltimore-city/bs-md-freddie-gray-lead-paint-20150423-story.html.

Martin, Charles H. "Internationalizing 'The American Dilemma': The Civil Rights Congress and the 1951 Genocide." *Journal of American Ethnic History* 16, no. 4 (1997): 35–61.

McLaughlin, Michael. "The Dynamic History of #BlackLivesMatter Explained." *Huffington Post,* December 26, 2016. www.huffingtonpost.com/entry/history-black-lives-matter_us_56d0a3b0e4b0871f60eb4af5.

McMurry, Evan. "CNN's Jones, Lemon Rip into Each Other over Ferguson Protests." *Mediaite,* November 25, 2014. www.mediaite.com/tv/cnns-jones-lemon-rip-into-each-other-over-ferguson-protests/.

Miller, Michael E. "Black Lives Matter Activist Kills Himself on Steps of Ohio Statehouse." *Washington Post,* February 9, 2016. www.washingtonpost.com/news/morning-mix/wp/2016/02/09/black-lives-matter-activist-kills-himself-on-steps-of-ohio-statehouse/.

Molloy, Mark, and Agencies. "Palestinians Tweet Tear Gas Advice to Protesters in Ferguson." *Telegraph,* August 15, 2014. www.telegraph .co.uk/news/worldnews/northamerica/usa/11036190/Palestinians-tweet-tear-gas-advice-to-protesters-in-Ferguson.html.

Moore, Darnell L. "Black Freedom Fighters in Ferguson: Some of Us Are Queer." *Feminist Wire,* October, 17, 2014. www.thefeministwire .com/2014/10/some-of-us-are-queer/.

Movement for Black Lives. "A Vision for Black Lives: Policy Demands for Black Power, Freedom and Justice." August 2016. https://policy. m4bl.org/.

Muhammad, Michael Z. "Black Radical Conference Connects Youth with Elders and the Struggle." *Final Call,* January 21, 2016. www.finalcall .com/artman/publish/National_News_2/article_102860.shtml.

Poe, Tef. "Dear Mr. President: A Letter from Tef Poe." *Riverfront Times,* December 1, 2014. www.riverfronttimes.com/musicblog/2014 /12/01/dear-mr-president-a-letter-from-tef-poe.

Prison Culture (blog). "#FireDanteServin: An Abolitionist Campaign in Chicago." September 19, 2015. www.usprisonculture.com/blog/2015/09 /19/firedanteservin-an-abolitionist-campaign-in-chicago/.

Rankin, Kenrya. "Baltimore Activists Protest Police Commissioner Appointment, Arrested during Sit-In." *Colorlines,* October 15, 2015. www.colorlines.com/articles/baltimore-activists-protest-police-commissioner-appointment-arrested-during-sit.

Ransby, Barbara. "Black Lives Matter Is Democracy in Action." *New York Times,* October 21, 2017.

———. "The Class Politics of Black Lives Matter." *Dissent,* Fall 2015.

———. "Ella Taught Me: Shattering the Myth of the Leaderless Movement." *Colorlines,* June 12, 2015. www.colorlines.com/articles /ella-taught-me-shattering-myth-leaderless-movement.

Ransby-Sporn, Asha. "MLK Day 2017: Mobilizing against Racism, Capitalism and Militarism in a Neo-fascist Era." *Truthout,* January 16, 2017. www.truth-out.org/opinion/item/39113-mlk-day-2017-mobilizing-against-racism-capitalism-and-militarism-in-a-neo-fascist-era.

Rector, Kevin, and Colin Campbell. "Protesters Occupy City Hall after Kevin Davis' Appointment Hearing." *Baltimore Sun,* October 15, 2015. www.baltimoresun.com/news/maryland/baltimore-city/bs-md-ci-davis-confirmation-hearing-20151014-story.html.

Robinson, Carol. "Black Protester Attacked at Donald Trump Rally Called 'Monkey' and Other Racial Slurs, He Claims." *AL.com,* updated October 18, 2016. www.al.com/news/birmingham/index .ssf/2015/11/black_protester_attacked_at_do.html.

Rogers, Jamala. "#Cutthecheck Is Not a Movement." *St. Louis American,* May 28, 2015. www.stlamerican.com/ferguson/cutthecheck-is-not-a-movement/article_b712cdc0-04e4-11e5-824b-83e71b951fc3.html.

Roland, Driadonna. "Sovereign Law Made Cliven Bundy a 'Patriot' but Korryn Gaines 'Crazy.'" *Revolt,* August 8, 2016. https://revolt.tv /stories/2016/08/08/sovereign-law-made-cliven-bundy-patriot-korryn-gaines-crazy-3517d33d30.

Rubbelke, Nathan. "Saint Louis University to Erect Monument Honoring Anti-police Protest." *College Fix,* February 3, 2015. www .thecollegefix.com/post/21099/.

Schmadeke, Steve. "Judge Who Has Heard High-Profile Cases Could Decide Officer Van Dyke's Fate." *Chicago Tribune,* December 29, 2015. www.chicagotribune.com/news/local/breaking/ct-jason-van-dyke-laquan-mcdonald-arraignment-20151229-story.html.

Sege, Adam. "Man Dies after Chicago Police Use Taser during Arrest." *Chicago Tribune,* May 21, 2014. www.chicagotribune.com /news/local/breaking/chi-man-tased-by-police-while-resisting-arrest-dies-20140521-story.html.

Selah, Umi. "Up You Mighty Race. Accomplish What You Will. What a Time. To Be Alive! What a Time. To Be Alive!" *Black Commentator* 637 (January 21, 2016). www.blackcommentator.com/637/637_up_ you_mighty_race_selah_guest.html.

Service Employees International Union. "Statement of SEIU President Mary Kay Henry on the Grand Jury Decision in Ferguson, Missouri." November 24, 2014. www.seiu.org/2014/11/statement-of-seiu-president-mary-kay-henry-on-the.

Sewell, Abby. "Activists Battle L.A. County Jailers' 'Culture of Violence.'" *Los Angeles Times,* April 14, 2014.

Sherwood, Courtney, and Kirk Johnson. "Bundy Brothers Acquitted in Takeover of Oregon Wildlife Refuge." *New York Times,* October 27,

2016. www.nytimes.com/2016/10/28/us/bundy-brothers-acquitted-in-takeover-of-oregon-wildlife-refuge.html?_r=o.

Smith, Mychal Denzel. "How Trayvon Martin's Death Launched a New Generation of Black Activism." *Nation,* September 15, 2014.

————. "The Rebirth of Black Rage." *Nation,* August 13, 2015.

Social Justice. "The History of Critical Resistance." Vol. 27, no. 3 (2000): 6–10.

Solomon, Akiba. "Chicago Woman Groped by Cop Found Innocent of Eavesdropping." *Colorlines,* August 29, 2011. www.colorlines.com/articles/chicago-woman-groped-cop-found-innocent-eavesdropping.

Speth, Gus. "System Change and Non-reformist Reforms." *Truthout,* October 15, 2015. www.truth-out.org/speakout/item/33255-system-change-and-non-reformist-reforms.

Stolberg, Sheryl Gay, and Jess Bidgood. "Some Women Won't 'Ever Again' Report a Rape in Baltimore." *New York Times,* August 11, 2016.

Swaine, Jon. "Ferguson Protester Faces Four Years' Jail over Charges of Kicking SUV." *Guardian,* August 12, 2015. www.theguardian.com/us-news/2015/aug/13/ferguson-protester-faces-four-years-jail-over-charges-of-attacking-suv-and-driver.

Taylor, G. Flint. "The Long Path to Reparations for the Survivors of Chicago Police Torture." *Northwestern Journal of Law & Social Policy,* vol. 11, no. 3 (Spring 2016). http://scholarlycommons.law.northwestern.edu/njlsp/vol11/iss3/1.

Tribune News Services. "Jury Convicts Man Who Wounded Black Lives Matter Protesters in Minnesota." *Chicago Tribune,* February 1, 2017. www.chicagotribune.com/news/nationworld/ct-black-lives-matter-protesters-shooting-verdict-20170201-story.html.

Truth, Sojourner. "Ain't I a Woman?" Speech delivered at the Women's Convention, Akron, Ohio, December 1851.

Uhuru, Lfe Johari. "'Occupy the Hood': Including All of the 99%." Interview by Jesse Strauss. *Al Jazeera,* October 10, 2011. www.aljazeera.com/indepth/features/2011/10/20111091910197087 86.html.

US Department of Justice. *Investigation of Ferguson Police Department.* Civil Rights Division. March 4, 2015.

————. *Investigation of the Baltimore City Police Department.* Civil Rights Division. August 10, 2016. www.justice.gov/opa/file/883366/download.

Viera, Bene. "How Activist (and ESSENCE Cover Star) Johnetta 'Netta' Elzie Speaks Her Truth and What It's Like Fighting for Yours." *Essence,* January 6, 2016. www.essence.com/2016/01/06/how-activist-and-essence-cover-star-johnetta-netta-elzie-speaks-her-truth-and-what-its.

Waldman, Amy. "The Truth about Jena." *Atlantic,* January/February 2008.

Wallsten, Peter. "The Rev. Jeremiah Wright Was an Early Concern, Obama Aide Admits." *Top of the Ticket* (blog). *Los Angeles Times,* March 16, 2008. http://latimesblogs.latimes.com/washington/2008/03/throughout-his.html.

Williams, Kale. "Alameda County D.A. Drops Charges against Black Friday 14." *SFGATE,* December 4, 2015. www.sfgate.com/bayarea/article/Alameda-County-DA-drops-against-Black-Friday-6675940.php.

Wortham, Jenna. "Black Tweets Matter." *Smithsonian Magazine,* September 2016. www.smithsonianmag.com/arts-culture/black-tweets-matter-180960117/.

Yancey, George, and Cornel West. "Cornel West: The Fire of a New Generation." *The Stone* (blog). *New York Times,* August 19, 2015. https://opinionator.blogs.nytimes.com/2015/08/19/cornel-west-the-fire-of-a-new-generation/.

FILMS AND TELEVISION SEGMENTS

Abdullah, Melina, and Nana Gyamfi. "Black Lives Matter Activist Convicted of 'Felony Lynching': 'It's More Than Ironic, It's Disgusting.'" In conversation with Amy Goodman and Nermeen Shaikh. Aired June 2, 2016, on *Democracy Now!* www.democracynow.org/2016/6/2/black_lives_matter_activist_convicted_of.

"Do Black Lives Matter? Robin DG Kelley and Fred Moten in Conversation." *Critical Resistance.* Aired January 8, 2015, on Vimeo, 1:25:36. https://vimeo.com/116111740.

DuVernay, Ava, dir. *13th*. Netflix. Kandoo Films, 2016.
Folayan, Sabaah, and Damon Davis, dirs. *Whose Streets?* New York: Magnolia Pictures, 2017.
Franco, Marisa. "Groups Express Solidarity after Michael Brown Shooting." Interview by Melissa Harris-Perry. *Melissa Harris-Perry Show*. Aired August 17, 2014, on MSNBC. www.msnbc.com/melissa-harris-perry/watch/groups-express-solidarity-after-shooting-318921795825.
———. "Latino Communities Must See Ferguson's Fight as Their Own." Interview by Melissa Harris-Perry. *Melissa Harris-Perry Show*. Aired August 20, 2014, on MSNBC. www.msnbc.com/melissa-harris-perry/latino-communities-must-see-fergusons-fight-their-own.
hampton, dream. *Treasure: From Tragedy to Trans Justice, Mapping a Detroit Story*. San Francisco: Frameline Distribution, 2015.
Love, Dayvon. "Continuing Activism after the Cameras Leave." Interview by Melissa Harris-Perry. *Melissa Harris-Perry Show*. Aired May 2, 2015, on MSNBC. www.msnbc.com/melissa-harris-perry/watch/continuing-activism-after-the-cameras-leave-438306883710.
Pool, Tim. "Ferguson: A Report from Occupied Territory." *Fusion*, March 30, 2015. On YouTube, 53:22. www.youtube.com/watch?v=gq9pHONmaLc.

INTERVIEWS BY THE AUTHOR

M. Adams, March 6, 2018, email.
Phillip Agnew, March 8, 2016, Chicago, Illinois.
Rasheed Aldridge, March 11, 2016, St. Louis, Missouri.
Nabeegah Azeri, March 12, 2016, St. Louis, Missouri.
Dante Barry, December 22, 2017, email.
Michaela Brown, December 15, 2017, email.
Charlene Carruthers, February 15, 2017, phone.
Cathy J. Cohen, December 3, 2017, email.
Kristiana Rae Colón, December 1, 2017, Chicago, Illinois.
Brittany Ferrell, September 4 and November 10, 2017, phone.
Alicia Garza, March 9, 2017, phone.

Brianna Gibson, November 2, 2017, email.

Rachel Gilmer, August 14, 2017, email.

Ash-Lee Henderson, March 10, 2018, email.

Julia Ho, March 12, 2016, St. Louis, Missouri.

Mariame Kaba, October 23, 2017, email.

Patrisse Khan-Cullors, February 15 and April 11, 2017, phone.

Alice Kim, December 26, 2017, email.

Derek Laney, March 12, 2016, St. Louis, Missouri.

Deana Lewis, April 20, 2017, email.

Dayvon Love, November 6, 2017, phone.

Page May, December 10, 2017, email.

Thenjiwe McHarris, October 26, 2017, phone.

Maurice (Moe) Mitchell, October 26, 2017, phone.

Aja Monet, March 8, 2016, Chicago, Illinois.

Jasson Perez, November 4, 2017, email.

Denise Perry, February 24, 2017, Franklinton, North Carolina.

Aislinn Pulley, February 4, 2018, email.

Asha Ransby-Sporn, February 8, 2017, email.

Kayla Reed, November 6, 2017, phone.

Beth E. Richie, December 8, 2017, email.

Andrea Ritchie, October 2, 2017, phone.

Jamala Rogers, March 12, 2016, St. Louis, Missouri.

Angie Rollins (Fresco Steez), December 19, 2017, email.

Alisha Sonnier, March 12, 2016, St. Louis, Missouri.

Todd St. Hill, November 16, 2017, Chicago, Illinois.

Opal Tometi, November 21 and 27, 2017, email.

Chinyere Tutashinda, January 8, 2018, email.

Elizabeth Vega, March 12, 2016, St. Louis, Missouri.